Crossway Bible Guide

Series Editors: Ian Coffey (NT), Stephen Gaukroger (OT)
New Testament Editor: Stephen Motyer

G4403

Dedicated to
Tim, Becky and Jon, three of the best.

Mark: Crossway Bible Guide
Free to follow Jesus

David Hewitt

Crossway Books
Leicester

ISBN 1-85684-118-9

Unless otherwise stated, Scripture quotations in this publication are
from the Holy Bible, New International Version. Copyright © 1973,
1978, 1984 International Bible Society. Published in Great Britain by
Hodder & Stoughton Ltd.

Typeset by Saxon Graphics Ltd, Derby.
Printed in Great Britain for Crossway Books, 38 De Montfort Street,
Leicester LE1 7GP, by Cox & Wyman Ltd, Reading, Berkshire.

Contents

Crossway Bible Guides

Series Editors' Introduction

Today, many groups of people meet together to study the Bible and this appears to be a booming leisure-time activity in many parts of the world. In the United Kingdom alone, over one million people each week meet in home Bible-study groups.

This series has been designed to help such groups and, in particular, those who lead them. We are also aware of the needs of those who preach and teach to larger groups as well as the hard-pressed student, all of whom often look for a commentary that gives a concise summary and lively application of a particular passage. We have tried to keep three clear aims in our sights:

1 To explain and apply the message of the Bible in non-technical language.

2 To encourage discussion, prayer and action on what the Bible teaches.

3 To enlist authors who are in the business of teaching the Bible to others and are doing it well.

All of us engaged in the project believe that the Bible is the Word of God – given to us in order that people might discover him and his purposes for our lives. We believe that the 66 books which go to make up the Bible, although written by different people, in different places, at different times, through different circumstances, have a single unifying theme: that theme is Salvation.

All of us hope that the books in this series will help people get a grip on the message of the Bible. But most important of all, we pray that the Bible will get a grip on you as a result!

Ian Coffey
Stephen Gaukroger
Series Editors

Note to readers

In our Bible Guides we have developed special symbols to make things easier to follow. Every passage therefore has an opening section which is the passage in a nutshell.

The main section is the one that makes sense of the passage.

Questions
Every passage also has special questions for group and personal study after the main section. Some questions are addressed to us as individuals, some speak to us as members of our church or home group, while others concern us as members of God's people worldwide.

Digging deeper
Some passages, however, require an extra amount of explanation, and we have put these sections into two categories. The first kind gives additional background material that helps us to understand something complex. For example, if we dig deeper into the Gospels, it helps us to know who the Pharisees were, so that we can see more easily why they related to Jesus in the way they did. These technical sections are marked with a spade.

Important doctrines
The second kind of background section appears with passages which have important doctrines contained in them, and which we need to study in more depth if we are to grow as Christians. Special sections that explain them to us in greater detail are marked with this symbol.

How to use this book

This book has been written on the assumption that it will be used in one of three ways:

- for individuals using it as an aid to personal study

- for groups wishing to use it as a study guide to Mark

- for those preparing to teach others.

The following guidelines will help you to get the most from the material.

Personal study

One of the best methods of Bible study is to read the text through carefully several times, possibly using different versions or translations. Having reflected on the material it is a good discipline to write down your own thoughts before doing anything else. At this stage the introduction of other books can be useful. If you are using this book as your main study resource, then read through the relevant sections carefully, turning up the Bible references that are mentioned. The questions at the end of each chapter are specifically designed to help you to apply the passage to your own situation. You may find it helpful to write your answers to the questions in your notes.

It is a good habit to conclude with prayer, bringing before God the things you have learned. If you follow the chapters of this book as a guide for studying Mark you will find it divides up into sixty-one separate studies of manageable length.

Group study

There are two choices:

a. You can take the fourteen main sections as weekly studies. These are of unequal length, divided according to the sense of the text, so you may wish to select sections that suit the length of your course.

b. You can opt for a selection of the sixty-one separate chapters, each featuring two or three study questions.

Members of the group should follow the guidelines set out above for *Personal study*. It is recommended that your own notes should contain:

a. Questions or comments on verses that you wish to discuss with the whole group.

b. Answers to the questions at the end of each section.

The format of your group time will depend on your leader, but it is suggested that the answers to the questions at the end of each section form a starting point for your discussions.

Teaching aid

If you are using this book as an aid to teaching others, note that the book of Mark has been divided into fourteen sections as follows:

The overture	1:1–13
The ministry gets under way	1:14–45
The conflict begins	2:1 – 3:6
Various reactions	3:7–35
Parables of the Kingdom	4:1–41
Acts of power	5:1 – 6:6
Jesus' discipleship training course	6:7–56
Breaking the mould	7:1 – 8:26
Shadow of the cross	8:27 – 9:50
Relationships in the Kingdom	10:1–52
The King takes charge	11:1 – 12:44
The King will return	13:1–37
Betrayed and denied	14:1–72
From Friday to Sunday	15:1 – 16:8

The divisions are not all of equal length but break up the text without destroying the flow of the teaching of the book. Each section contains chapters (never more than four per section) which deal with the key points of the text. If fourteen sessions are too many for your course you can omit some and/or merge some of the shorter ones. The questions at the end of each chapter can easily be adapted for group use.

Acknowledgments

Special thanks to Phyllis Funnell for transferring my incomprehensible scrawl into a presentable manuscript. Also to Jenny Greenwood and Rosemary Sabroe for help in this time-consuming task.

General thanks to the members of Andover Baptist Church for helpful comments and suggestions as they studied Mark's gospel in house groups.

Particular thanks to Rev. Peter Barber, who died during the writing of this book and with whom I first shared a series of sermons in this thrilling gospel at Upton Vale Baptist Church, Torquay, in the 1970s.

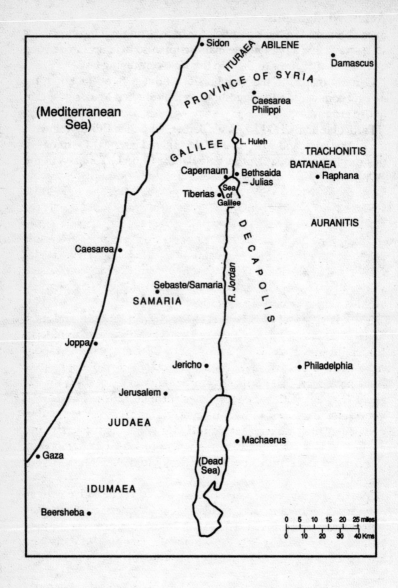

Palestine in the time of Jesus

Introduction

'If you came from a strange planet and didn't know anything about God, then I would say "read Mark's gospel".' 'It's the nearest we will ever get to an eyewitness account of Jesus.' 'Mark tells the story in a way that I can understand.'

These were just some of the comments from members of a house group as they looked back over their time studying Mark's gospel. New church-goers and those who had been Christians for many years all spoke about what they had gained. 'Here' said one, 'we see that God not only said it but did it.'

Mark is a gospel of action. It is the earliest, briefest and most direct account we have of the life, death and resurrection of Jesus Christ. Readers in the United Kingdom will be aware of the various daily newspapers available. Mark is the *Daily Mirror* of the gospels! Bold headlines, brief articles, simple language. If you want *The Daily Telegraph* with a conservative slant then turn to Matthew. If you prefer *The Guardian* with its concern for the poor and under-privileged then Luke is for you. If you want the reflection and analysis of *The Times* then John is where to look. But if you want the basic story, simply and convincingly told then Mark is your gospel.

Mark's gospel has been described as 'a passion narrative with an introduction', because half of his sixteen chapters are concerned with the events of the last period of Jesus' ministry. The turning point is found in Mark 8:27–30, when Peter confesses to Jesus 'You are the Christ'. Everything has been leading up to this moment of recognition.

From Caesarea Philippi the road leads straight to the cross. 'He then began to teach them that the Son of Man must suffer many things ... and that he must be killed ...' (8:31)

The climax of the second part comes at the cross itself when a Roman centurion says in words deeper than he understood 'Surely this man was the Son of God!' (15:39).

So what does Mark want us to see? In the first half we will see how Jesus' ministry develops – there will be preaching and teaching, healing and miracles, witnessing and opposition. Everything begs the question – just who is this man? In the second half the road narrows, the crowds slip away, the path leads very quickly to the cross. We will watch him die, betrayed, forsaken, alone. But Mark will finally reassure us that this is not the end. The cross is empty and so is the tomb. 'He has risen!' (16:6) Mark's whole aim is not to write a biography but to paint a portrait of 'Jesus Christ, the Son of God'. Someone who is worth following as much today as in the dark and dangerous days when Mark wrote his exciting gospel.

'It could be argued that Mark's gospel is the most important book ever written' (William Barclay).

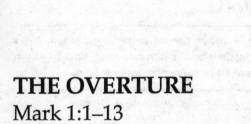

THE OVERTURE
Mark 1:1–13

Like John, Mark omits the events of Bethlehem and plunges straight into his story. In these opening verses several important themes are introduced that will be developed later.

Mark 1:1–8

A signpost to Jesus

The story that Mark is about to tell centres on Jesus. Mark introduces him to us in the very first verse, then tells us about the person who was sent to prepare the way for him.

 Mark's gospel begins with a fanfare! The good news starts here! The opening verse is both a title for the book and a summary of its contents. His aim is to introduce us to Jesus. Unlike the other gospel writers, he is straight into the action. Mark's gospel was written in a hurry. The storm clouds of persecution were gathering over the young Christian church. A great fire had devastated two-thirds of the city of Rome in AD 64: of the fourteen wards of the city only four were spared. Three were totally destroyed. The flames raged unchecked for more than a week. Who was responsible? The rumour began to spread that the emperor Nero, himself, had started the blaze. He had earlier proposed a massive rebuilding project for the city but his plans had been rejected. The fire seemed too much of a coincidence – had Nero taken phase one of the rebuilding programme into his own hands? A scapegoat had to be found. Nero pointed the finger at the Christians. They were responsible, it was said; they must be arrested, imprisoned, executed. Life became very dangerous for God's people in Rome. (The situation is reflected in Peter's first letter.)

In the persecution that followed, it is thought that both Peter and Paul lost their lives. The issue was brought to a head – the facts about the life, teaching, death and resurrection of Jesus had to be written down. And written down quickly before all those who had known Jesus in person lost their lives. Mark was given the task.

We can sense the tense atmosphere in the way Mark writes. The whole gospel throbs with life and movement. Two out of every three verses begin with the word 'and'! Over forty times he uses the word 'immediately'. It is a matter of urgency.

Mark introduces John the Baptist to us with a quotation from the Old Testament. This is unusual for Mark, unlike Matthew's gospel, written originally for Jews, which is full of such quotations. But Mark is keen to show that although what God is doing is something exciting and new, it is the fulfilment of all that has gone before. John is the human link-piece between the Old and New Testament.

The voice of the prophet had been silent in Israel for over 300 years, but now, as promised, God's messenger had come. His unusual dress would have reminded people of Elijah, the prophet who was to come just before the Messiah. John was a man with burning convictions and an uncompromising message. He was calling people back to God.

Crowds gathered from miles around to hear him. Some probably came out of curiosity, but many others knew that their lives were not right before God. They needed forgiveness. Their baptism was an outward sign of their repentance. In the past only Gentiles (that is, non-Jews) had been baptised but now God was calling his own people to a new relationship with himself.

Inevitably speculation arose – who was this fiery preacher? Was he the promised Messiah? John is quick to squash any such ideas.

The heart of his message is about someone else, that is, Jesus. John feels he is not worthy to do even a slave's work for him. John's task is to prepare the way and then get out of the way! Like a pacemaker in an athletics race, he is there to set the pace for the first few laps and then slip quietly off the track. John is a signpost to Jesus. Something we are all called to be.

Questions

1. What do these opening verses indicate about Mark's purpose in writing his gospel?
2. Why do you think so many people came to listen to John the Baptist?
3. What can we learn from John the Baptist about pointing people to Jesus Christ? What things can prevent us from being effective 'signposts to Jesus'?

Mark

It is generally accepted that the writer of Mark's gospel is the John Mark we read of elsewhere in the New Testament. John was his Hebrew name, but he is more usually known by his later name, Mark.

He was someone who was particularly well qualified to write the story of Jesus. A Jewish Christian born and bred in Jerusalem, his mother kept open house for the early Christians. After his release from prison Peter made straight for this home (Acts 12:12). It was probably a regular meeting place for fellowship and worship. It may even have been in the upstairs room of John Mark's home that Jesus shared the last supper with his disciples. Many think that the unusual reference to a young man in Mark 14:51 is Mark's own way of saying 'I was there'. The incident is not recorded by Matthew or Luke.

The sorry story of Mark the missionary is recorded in Acts. Accompanying Paul and Barnabas, his uncle, on the first missionary journey (Acts 12:25) the trip became too much for him and he returned to Jerusalem (13:13). The hardest and most dangerous part of the journey lay ahead. Mark turned back. It is encouraging to think that God used someone who had failed, to write this exciting gospel.

Mark may not have reached many people as a conventional missionary, but thousands have been introduced to Jesus through his gospel. Although details are lacking, Paul was later reconciled to Mark. He is with Paul during his imprisonment in Rome (Philemon 24) and acts as his representative on a mission to Asia Minor (Colossians 4:10). Paul describes him as useful to him (2 Timothy 4:11). When 1 Peter is written, Mark is in Rome with Peter who describes him affectionately as his son (1 Peter 5:13).

Isaiah the prophet

Although Mark writes of Isaiah (verse 2) the quotations, in fact, come from Malachi and Exodus as well as Isaiah (Malachi 3:1; Exodus 23:20; Isaiah 40:3). Some think that Mark was using a translation which wrongly attributed these verses to Isaiah. It is more likely, however, that this is a collection of Old Testament sayings that had already been drawn together because of their common theme. Mark puts Isaiah's name to them because he is the best known of the authors. Isaiah was the most well-loved and widely-read of the prophets in Jesus' time.

A baptism of repentance

Ritual washing was a familiar part of Jewish religious practice. Leviticus chapters 11 to 15, give instruction for such rituals. But to call God's people to a baptism of repentance was something new. If a Gentile wanted to become a Jew then he had to undergo two rites. Firstly, he had to be circumcised, for this was the mark of God's covenant people, and then baptism, which symbolised his cleansing from all the pollution of his past life. Such a convert was called a proselyte.

John was calling Jews to submit to something that in the past only a Gentile was considered to require. John's message was revolutionary. They were not to rely on their religious heritage but needed to make a fresh commitment to God.

Repentance means to change direction. John was calling his listeners to turn away from wrongdoing and to turn back to God. It was a message that the prophets in Israel had regularly preached and was one that Jesus would take up as his ministry began (verse 15).

Mark 1:9–13

Necessary preparations

Before Jesus' campaign gets under way, he is baptised by John and empowered by the Holy Spirit for the task ahead. Immediately the genuineness of Jesus' call is tested.

Jesus is already some thirty years of age when he first appears in Mark's story (Luke 3:23). Mark is not interested in writing a detailed biography of Jesus' life, rather, his aim is to present to us the significant events of Jesus' ministry.

Quietly Jesus enters the stage as one of the crowd coming to John the Baptist to be baptised. Nazareth has been his home during these hidden years of growth and development (see John 1:46). He would have received an elementary education, studied the Jewish scriptures and worked alongside his father, Joseph, in the carpenter's shop. But now the waiting time was over. God's time has come. It was time for Jesus' brief ministry to begin.

It may surprise us that the one whom we understand to be sinless should come to a baptism that was for those who needed forgiveness (see verse 4). Matthew, in his gospel, records how reluctant John was to baptise Jesus (Matthew 3:13–14). We can understand John's hesitancy. The clue to understanding why Jesus was baptised is in the word 'identification'.

Firstly, Jesus was identifying with the message and ministry of John the Baptist. Jesus was giving his seal of approval to all that John had been saying and doing. But secondly, and at a deeper level, Jesus was identifying with sinful men and women. It was the first step on his journey to the cross, where he would be fully 'numbered with the transgressors' in Isaiah's words (Isaiah 53:12). The one who was to baptise with the Holy Spirit comes to the baptism of sinners as their representative. His baptism was the beginning of the costly identification that culminated in his death on the cross (2 Corinthians 5:21).

As Jesus came up out of the water the sky was 'torn open'. The word Mark uses is a violent one that was used of ripping a cloth in two, from which we get our word 'schism'. It was the answer to Isaiah's longing that God would 'rend the heavens and come down' (Isaiah 64:1). But in vivid contrast to the violent tearing, a gentle dove descends. God's Spirit, that can be likened to wind and fire, can also be pictured as a dove. Mark *begins* and *ends* with a *tearing* (1:10; 15:38) and a voice confessing this sonship (1:11; 15:39).

The voice from heaven (it seems likely that others would have heard it as well as Jesus) is thought to bring together two Old Testament images of the coming Messiah. 'You are my Son' is an echo of Psalm 2:7 and 'in whom I am well pleased' reflects Isaiah 42:1. Neither is an exact quotation, but we can see here a combining of the royal king of the Psalms and the suffering servant of Isaiah. Jesus is both the King who reigns and the Saviour who suffers.

At his baptism Jesus is commissioned and empowered for his ministry. Then the battle begins! Immediately his calling is tested.

This is also a necessary part of his preparation. The same Spirit who descends on him at the River Jordan now drives him into the desert! Mark's account is strikingly brief, the other gospel writers give us more details. For nearly six weeks Jesus undergoes a severe testing in a dangerous and lonely place. But God's angels are with him.

Having passed through this experience Jesus' ministry can begin.

Questions

1. How do the events surrounding Jesus' baptism prepare him for the temptations that follow? What do you think is the significance of the presence of the animals and the angels? (Note: Many Christians in Mark's day were facing wild animals in the Roman arena.) Are there any parallels for us today?

2. Why do you think that Jesus had to undergo such a severe examination before he could begin his ministry? Does God sometimes take us through similar times of testing?

3. What encouragement can you draw from verses 12–13, when you are faced with temptation? (See Hebrews 4:15)

2

THE MINISTRY
GETS UNDER WAY
Mark 1:14—45

Powerfully, Jesus calls his first followers, drives out evil spirits and heals the sick. These were the halcyon days for Jesus and his disciples, brief but precious.

Mark 1:14–20

The ministry begins

Although the imprisonment of John the Baptist is the human time switch, more importantly, God's special time has come. But it all starts in the most unlikely place and with the most unlikely people!

Galilee, Peter's home district, was frowned upon by the Jews of Jesus' day. It was considered unfashionable and very much downmarket. People from Galilee were noted for their slovenly speech: Peter was immediately recognisable by his local accent (Mark 14:70). Obscure and despised, predominantly Gentile, Galilee was a long way from Jerusalem, the centre of Jewish life, in more ways than one. Yet this was God's place (see Isaiah 9:1–2).

Jesus' message is direct and compelling: 'It's time to turn back to God'. The Kingdom of God is at the threshold of people's lives. This is God's time. Such a message demands a response – the kind of response we see demonstrated by the four fishermen who were prepared to drop everything and follow Jesus.

Disciples were a common feature of Jesus' day. A number of pupils would attach themselves to a rabbi or teacher whose message appealed to them. The unusual feature here is that Jesus chose his disciples and not the other way round.

Fishermen were also common in Galilee. Josephus, the Jewish historian says that in his day as many as 330 fishing boats sailed the lake. Fish was the staple diet for ordinary people who could rarely afford meat. Fishermen would have been by nature or experience, brave, strong, patient men who were not afraid of hard and uncomfortable work.

It is striking that Jesus chose such ordinary men (see Acts 4:13) and not the intellectual, well-taught religious leaders. They were not stupid but neither were they special. They were just ordinary. It is an illustration of the principle Paul gives later in the New Testament about God choosing the foolish and the weak (1 Corinthians 1:26–31). Church history also demonstrates the same principle, for example, John Bunyan, the tinker, who wrote *The Pilgrim's Progress*; William Carey, the cobbler, founder of the modern missionary movement; and William Booth, the pawnbroker's assistant, who founded the Salvation Army.

These fishermen were probably in their late teens or early twenties. Jesus sometimes refers to them as 'children' or even 'little children' (one translation records this as 'lads').

Paul, writing much later (around AD 55) records that many of the first disciples were still alive (1 Corinthians 15:6). Christianity began as a youth movement.

It is interesting to note also that they were actively involved in their daily business when Jesus called them. Simon and Andrew were fishing close to the shore, whilst James and John were mending their broken nets. Like Moses keeping sheep, Gideon threshing wheat, Elisha ploughing and Amos working as a herdsman, God's call came to those who were busy in their every-day occupation.

Mark has no time to give us the background, but John, in his gospel (1:35–42) indicates that they had met Jesus before. It is possible that they had become disciples of John the Baptist.

Whatever preparation there may have been, we are still struck by the immediate and total response they made to Jesus' call. They were prepared to sever their secular and domestic ties to follow Christ.

Why did Jesus call them? Because he had a purpose for them – to reach others with the good news of the Kingdom. He promises to make them into something they could not possibly make themselves. They will be using their old fishing skills to catch men.

Questions

1. What exactly was the good news that Jesus proclaimed (verses 14, 15)? Was it just about forgiveness? What sort of response does he invite? How did you react when you were first challenged with it? What do you think Jesus meant by the 'Kingdom of God'?

2. Why do you think that the first people Jesus called to follow him were ordinary men and not from among the religious leaders of the day? Should we expect a more ready response to the gospel from those on a lower social level?

3. What factors might have contributed to the ready response of the four fishermen? Does their response surprise you? Does Jesus ask for the same kind of radical obedience from us? Do we need to give up work to follow Jesus? Is that Mark's message?

The Kingdom of God

Jesus' message concerned the 'Kingdom of God'. We find the phrase fourteen times in Mark's gospel and over one hundred times in all four gospels. It is here in his first recorded message and in his last messages according to Acts 1:3.

Jesus' parables were parables of the Kingdom. What did Jesus mean by this? Is it a future Kingdom? Is it the church? What does it have to do with us today?

At the time of Jesus, the idea of the Kingdom was common in Jewish thinking. Scholars looked forward to a new age of peace and material well-being when Israel would be free from the oppression of Rome. Increasingly the phrase, the Kingdom of God, had taken on a highly political tone. It had become virtually a slogan for Jewish nationalism. Political activists and freedom fighters had begun to take things into their own hands. Such revolutionaries were called 'zealots' (Jesus chose one among his disciples – Mark 3:18). Galilee, in particular, became a hotbed for such men. We can easily imagine the tension in the air, therefore, when Jesus proclaimed 'The kingdom of God is near!'. But Jesus' understanding of the Kingdom was different in a number of ways.

● Firstly, for Jesus the Kingdom was not national but personal. It was about God's rule in a person's heart. The Kingdom was not a territory to be found on a map (like the United Kingdom) but God's reign as King in an individual's life. During his trial, Jesus explains to Pontius Pilate that his Kingdom is 'not of this world' (John 18:36). It's another kind of Kingdom.

● Secondly, for Jesus the Kingdom was not material but spiritual. It is not a place of earthly prosperity but spiritual blessing. When

Jesus was asked by some Pharisees when the Kingdom would come, he told them that the Kingdom of God is 'within you'. That is, it is an internal and spiritual Kingdom not an external and visible one (Luke 17:21). Paul, later in the New Testament, tells us in Romans 14:17 that 'the kingdom of God is not a matter of eating and drinking, but of righteousness, peace and joy in the Holy Spirit'.

● Thirdly, for Jesus the Kingdom was not only future but here and now. With the coming of Jesus, God's rule among men had begun. The day the prophets had dreamed of was here. The Kingdom was here because Jesus was here!

And now, whenever a person receives Christ as Lord, by repentance and faith, the Kingdom of God is present, for they have made God King in their lives. Undoubtedly, there is a future element to the Kingdom of God. The Bible looks forward to a time when 'the kingdom of the world has become the kingdom of our Lord and of his Christ' (Revelation 11:15). But the first stage is here. Hence the challenge to repent and believe, for this is the way into God's Kingdom.

Mark 1:21–34

A day in the life of Jesus

Mark gives us a summary of what may have been a typical day in Jesus' busy schedule during the early months of his ministry in Galilee.

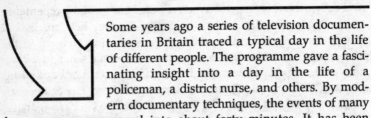

Some years ago a series of television documentaries in Britain traced a typical day in the life of different people. The programme gave a fascinating insight into a day in the life of a policeman, a district nurse, and others. By modern documentary techniques, the events of many hours were compressed into about forty minutes. It has been suggested that Mark is doing something very similar in this passage – giving us in just thirteen verses, a day in the life of Jesus.

The narrative moves rapidly from scene to scene. It begins in the synagogue, then moves to a home and then into the village streets. Attention focuses on a congregation, then an individual and then a crowd. The account buzzes with drama and activity. Verses 21–28 give us the morning, verses 29–31 the afternoon and verses 32–34 the evening.

The day begins with a walk down from Nazareth on the side of the hill to the lakeside town of Capernaum. Situated on the northwest banks of Galilee, Capernaum was an important, bustling community. On the main road between Egypt and Damascus it was a customs post and the Jewish capital of the region. A flourishing centre for fish and agriculture, it became something of a new headquarters for Jesus.

As it is the Sabbath, Jesus, accompanied by his first followers (Simon, Andrew, James and John), attends the synagogue service. His reputation has gone before him and he is invited to preach. What Jesus said, we do not know, but what remained in Peter's memory, as he recalled it to Mark, was the reaction of the people.

The word Mark uses in verse 22 expresses their amazement mingled with a level of uncertainty, even fear. Jesus' teaching is refreshing and new, but also challenging and disturbing.

The quietness of the synagogue is broken by the sudden cry of a man possessed by an evil spirit (see *Evil spirits* p. 33). This man, in the grip of a power outside himself, recognises who Jesus is and what he has come to do (see 1 John 3:8). Jesus cuts him short. There is a further gasp of amazement as one whom the people had probably considered incurable is set free. They wonder just what is happening amongst them.

The scene moves rapidly from the public synagogue to a private home where Jesus confronts another kind of evil – disease. Simon's mother-in-law lay sick, possibly with malaria which was common in this damp lakeside area. When Jesus is told about it, he acts again with great simplicity and quiet authority. Gently he raises her to her feet and the one who was so ill a few minutes before busies herself preparing a meal. The healing is instant and complete. There is no trace of weakness.

When the sun sets the Sabbath is over. The Jewish Sabbath lasted from sunset Friday to sunset Saturday and during that time no work was to be done, no burden was to be carried. The evening hours of this tiring day are the busiest of all.

The word has spread and it seems as if the entire population of Capernaum has gathered outside the house. Jesus moves among the crowd giving healing and exorcism. It must have been a thrilling occasion for the people of the area and an exhausting one for Jesus. But Jesus' bed is empty early the next morning as he slips away to spend time with his heavenly Father (verse 35).

Questions

1. Why do you think Jesus told the evil spirits to be quiet about who he was? (See also 1:44) Is demon possession a reality today?
2. Imagine you were Simon Peter – relive the 'day' through his eyes. Describe your feelings at each stage and at the end of the day. What impressions of Jesus would be forming in your mind?
3. Jesus' authority is clearly demonstrated in this passage. Compare Jesus' use of authority with that of other authorities of our time. What can we learn from Jesus about the proper exercise of authority?

Synagogue worship

The synagogue is the place where Jews met to worship. The Jewish faith centred on the Temple in Jerusalem, but through force of circumstances, first the exile and later the scattered Jewish communities, the local synagogue became for all practical purposes the centre of Jewish life. The law prescribed that wherever there were ten Jewish families, there should be a synagogue. At the time of Jesus, there were nearly 500 in Jerusalem alone.

Synagogue worship was relatively simple with the emphasis on teaching and instruction. Unlike most church services today there was no music or singing and the service had just three main elements – prayer, the reading of the Scriptures and its exposition. There was no professional ministry and, therefore, any man who was able to, might be invited to speak. It would have been quite natural for Jesus to be given the opportunity to occupy the teacher's chair.

The affairs of the synagogue were administered by 'the ruler of the synagogue'. In a large congregation there would be several such people (see Acts 13:15). An 'attendant' (Luke 4:20) was responsible for taking out and storing away the sacred rolls of Scripture.

He also acted as caretaker, cleaning the synagogue and carrying out several other responsibilities, such as teaching the children. The 'teachers of the law' who often did the teaching were recognised experts in the Old Testament Law or 'Torah', that is, the first five books of the Old Testament. They sought to extract from God's Law rules and regulations for every possible situation. These 'laws' were never written down and became known as the 'Oral Tradition'. Their teaching would be an exposition of these many rules and regulations. For their authority they would appeal to this oral tradition. They would repeatedly quote the teachers of the past: 'Rabbi so and so says this ... Rabbi such and such says that ...' Their teaching was deliberately unoriginal. They rarely gave personal views or independent judgments.

How different Jesus was! He quoted no authorities and cited no experts. His teaching was fresh and rang with personal authority. No wonder the people were amazed, just as they were by his miracles.

Evil spirits

The 'authority' of Jesus was the thing that amazed the people of Capernaum. The authority was displayed by what he did as well as by what he said (verses 22, 27). In these verses Jesus demonstrates his authority over evil spirits and disease.

'Evil spirits' were very much part of the world view of first-century Jews. There were, according to some, 7½ million of them, every person having 10,000 on his right and 10,000 on his left. They were thought to live in unclean places like the desert or among the tombs. There were many exorcists who with elaborate and extended rituals tried to set people free.

Although some would dismiss evil spirits as belonging to the sphere of primitive thought, several things should be borne in mind. Firstly, the gospel writers make a clear distinction between possession and illness. There is no suggestion, for example, that Simon Peter's mother-in-law's illness was the result of an evil spirit. The two conditions are differentiated by Mark in verse 34. Again, throughout the gospel, Mark records the striking difference between the forms of address to Jesus used by those under the influence of evil spirits and ordinary sick people. Whereas those who are unwell use terms like 'Son of David' (10:47, 48) and 'Rabbi' (10:51), the possessed use much fuller descriptions e.g. 'the Holy One of God' (1:24), 'Son of God' (3:11) or 'Son of the Most High God' (5:7). Indicating, at the very least, that they were in Mark's eyes in a different category from those who were simply unwell. Their recognition of Jesus is not a confession of faith but a defensive attempt to gain control of Jesus.

Contemporary testimony from many parts of the world speaks of the continuing reality of evil spirits and the power of Jesus to deliver. Although some situations may be considered psychological or a case of mistaken diagnosis, we dare not dismiss both biblical and contemporary evidence lightly.

What shines through from Mark's account is the undeniable authority of Jesus.

There is no elaborate ritual involved, just a simple word of command, literally, 'Be muzzled'! (J.B. Phillips confessed to being tempted to translate it, 'Belt up!', but he settled for 'Hold your tongue!') It is a powerful command and the evil spirits are powerless to resist. We shall see this authority demonstrated again later in the gospel (e.g. 5:1–20).

Mark 1:35–45

Jesus does and says surprising things

Surprisingly, Jesus turns his back on a promising situation. He will not be directed by public demand but by God's purpose for him.

The heavy demands of the previous day's ministry made prayer all the more vital for Jesus. Mark tells us that it was 'very early' and 'still dark' when Jesus got up. It was probably between three and four in the morning.

This is one of only three occasions of Jesus at prayer recorded in Mark's gospel. The other incidents are after the feeding of the five thousand (6:46) and in the garden of Gethsemane (14:32–42). These are critical moments in Jesus' ministry. Always the issue at stake, namely, what kind of Messiah is he going to be – a popular healer and feeder of men and women or a Saviour who suffers and dies? Surely Jesus felt the pull of popularity and success. It is not easy to leave a place of effective ministry and excellent prospects in order to break new ground.

While everyone was looking for him, Jesus was seeking his Father. He needed to restore his strength and his perspective. Although Jesus loved the crowd, he was not going to let them squeeze out his quiet place with God or dictate his strategy.

Simon Peter leads the search party who track him down. He is keen that they should carry on where they left off yesterday. Capernaum was ready and waiting for more. Jesus refuses to go back; rather, he says, 'We must go on to other places'. The word Mark uses is a specific one for large agricultural villages which had the size of a city but the structure of a village. Galilee was full of such 'villages' in Jesus' day.

Jesus' phrase, 'That is why I have come' (verse 38), appears to be deliberately ambiguous. It could refer to his leaving Capernaum or at a deeper level his coming from heaven. Jesus' primary purpose was not to heal and deliver but to preach the message of the Kingdom. Although healing was an integral part of his mission, Jesus deliberately interrupts the miracles to go elsewhere to preach. It is interesting to note that there is no reference to healing in verse 39. His miracles were illustrations of his message. (John in his gospel calls them 'signs'.)

The miracle that Mark then recounts is an example of this. Jesus heals a man suffering from leprosy. His condition would have made him not only physically unwell but a social and religious outcast. Lepers were unloved and unwanted. Onlookers would have been shocked to see Jesus touch the man.

The motivation for Jesus' action was compassion, although some manuscripts say that he was 'moved with anger'. If this is true we are not to think that he was angry with the man but with the disease that had so ravaged and disfigured his life. Perhaps there is also anger at the way those suffering from leprosy were being rejected and mistreated.

But the story then takes another strange twist as Jesus tells the man, in no uncertain terms, not to tell anyone about what has happened. The expression Mark uses is a strong one meaning a snort or groan. It represents deep emotion, almost as if Jesus regrets what he has just done. Had his compassion outweighed his caution? Unfortunately, the man takes no notice of Jesus' stern warning and his well-meaning enthusiasm proves a hindrance to Jesus' continuing ministry in that area.

It was normal practice for a healed person to present themselves before the priest. He would verify the healing and open the way back into the community for the former outcast.

Jesus knew the man would have to tell somebody and this would be a powerful testimony against the religious leaders when the time came. It was evidence of the new thing God was doing among them.

Questions

1. Why do you think it was important for Jesus to spend time in prayer at this particular time? What does this tell us about his priorities? How can we ensure that prayer does not get squeezed out of our day when we are really busy?

2. Are you surprised by Jesus' strategy in verse 38? What would have been the advantages/disadvantages in going back to Capernaum?

3. 'Holy' people were expected to keep away from 'sinners'. Jesus took a totally different line, he touched this man. What type of people do you feel most uncomfortable associating with? Who are the 'lepers' of society today? How can we show the same kind of compassion as Jesus did?

Leprosy

Although the term leprosy is usually confined today to what is known as Hansen's disease, in the Bible it is used to cover a wide variety of skin diseases. Seven distinct varieties are mentioned in Leviticus 13 and 14 together with regulations as to how those suffering with the disease were to be treated. 'The person with such an infectious disease must wear torn clothes, let his hair be unkempt, cover the lower part of his face and cry out, "Unclean, Unclean!" … He must live alone; he must live outside the camp.' (Leviticus 13:45–46)

Rabbis had refined these regulations to make life even more unhappy and isolated. A chance encounter with a leprosy sufferer would render the other person unclean. If a sufferer entered a house it would be considered unclean. A screen was provided in the synagogue to separate leprosy sufferers from the rest of the congregation. Many people regarded the disease as a punishment for sin. It is hard for us to grasp the horror and revulsion leprosy caused among people in these days, the mental anguish and social stigma multiplied the physical suffering.

If a leprosy sufferer was cured, he had to undergo a complicated ceremony of restoration. It is described in Leviticus 14 and involved a number of sacrifices and several examinations. Only after such an ordeal was the sufferer allowed to leave with a certificate to prove that he was clean.

Jesus' response to leprosy was wonderfully new. He stretched out his hand not to push the man away but in a compassionate touch. It was probably the first time the man had been touched by another person for many years. In an act of unheard-of compassion, Jesus was quite prepared to break ceremonial law in order to reach out to a person in need. Jesus was not made 'unclean' by the encounter, rather the man was made 'clean'.

Why the silence?

We are surprised when we read Jesus' strong words to the man he has healed. Why should he not share the story of what Jesus has done? He had a powerful testimony to tell.

There were probably a number of reasons why Jesus told him to keep quiet. Firstly, an open testimony would have misrepresented Jesus. He did not want to be known merely as a healer, this was not the primary ministry he had come to fulfil. We have seen earlier in this section how Jesus turned his back on a healing situation in order to go elsewhere to preach. For Jesus the miracles were secondary to the message.

Secondly, an open testimony at this stage would have led to a superficial response from the people. As in Capernaum, people would have come simply for healing without any real understanding of repentance and faith.

Thirdly, an open testimony would have hindered Jesus' ministry. And this is precisely what happened. The man's disobedience prevented Jesus' free movement and he is forced to withdraw to the desert again.

It is worth noting that Jesus apparently heals less and less as his ministry goes on. His healing miracles were real but secondary, they were testimony to his message. When he healed the blind, he was demonstrating his ability to open people's eyes to God. When he healed the deaf, he was demonstrating his power to open people's ears to God's work. When he healed the man with leprosy, he was demonstrating his compassion for the unwanted and unloved.

THE CONFLICT BEGINS

3

Mark 2:1 – 3:6

We are not too far into Jesus' ministry before the opposition begins. In this section Mark records five incidents that all have the elements of conflict in them, culminating in the threat to kill him (3:6). The shadow of the cross can already be seen.

Mark 2:1–12

Jesus' power to forgive

In this passage Jesus performs a miracle everybody can see, the healing of a man who cannot walk, in order to demonstrate that he is also able to perform a miracle we cannot see, that is, to forgive sins.

The religious leaders of the day took offence at Jesus on three grounds:

- The claims he made – notably to forgive sins (2:7)

- The company he kept – eating with tax collectors and sinners (2:16)

- The customs he disregarded – fasting (2:18) and Sabbath observance (2:24).

It was not that Jesus deliberately provoked opposition but the religious authorities found him altogether far too radical and threatening.

The scene is once more in Capernaum, possibly in the home of Simon Peter. The news has spread that Jesus is there and a great crowd of people gather to hear him. They fill the one-room house and spill out into the street. Whilst Jesus is preaching four men arrive carrying their friend who is unable to walk on a mattress, the common bed for an ordinary man. They are not able to get anywhere near Jesus because of the crowd, but such is their loyalty and determination that they are not so easily beaten.

The house would have had a flat roof made of light materials such as straw and earth spread across rafters and there would have been an outside staircase. Perhaps they had seen coffins taken in or out of the house in this way. Quickly they climb the stairs and begin, literally, in Mark's words, to 'deroof the roof'. We can imagine pieces of mud and straw beginning to fall on the people below. Undeterred, they continue until the hole is large enough to lower their friend through to the feet of Jesus.

Jesus sees their determined action and their ingenuity as a powerful demonstration of their faith in his ability to help their friend. Whether the man on the bed shared their faith we cannot be sure. Maybe he was in such a state of despair over his condition and so weighed down by his guilt that he had to rely on the faith of others. Were it not for his friends this man would never have reached the healing presence of Jesus.

Jesus' reaction is surprising. Was he aware of deeper causes for this man's condition? At first his words seem irrelevant, 'Son, your sins are forgiven'. The Jews saw an unbreakable link between sickness and sin (see p. 42). That Jesus did not share such a direct equation between sin and suffering is illustrated in various gospel incidents (e.g. Luke 13:1–5; John 9:1–7). But he had come from God to confront evil in all its forms. Sickness, disease and death are all consequences of mankind's sinful condition and it is this condition that Jesus came to deal with. He was concerned not so much with the symptoms as the root cause of things. Jesus bypasses all the normal requirements of the day, for forgiveness – a visit to the Temple to offer a sacrifice, making restitution, etc.

The teachers of the law (see p. 43) are understandably upset. Their response is a perfectly proper one. Only the offended party can forgive the offender, therefore, only God can forgive sin. Consequently, Jesus was guilty of blasphemy and the punishment for blasphemy was death by stoning. There was, of course, an alternative explanation, but their eyes were blind to it. Namely, that Jesus could speak for God because he was God Incarnate.

Although their concerns are not voiced, Jesus is nevertheless aware of them and he confronts them with a pointed question. 'Which is easier? ... (verse 9). In one sense it would be easier to say 'Your sins are forgiven' as there would be no way of telling whether it had happened or not. But to pronounce healing would be something everyone would be aware of. So Jesus, taking on his opponents on their own terms, performs a miracle that they can see in order that they might know that he had also performed the miracle they could not see. The reality of the healing demonstrates the reality of the forgiveness. Both forgiveness and healing are marks of the Kingdom of God among men.

Immediately the man is healed and the mattress that formerly carried him he now carries. The sign of his weakness is now a symbol of his new-found strength. Once more everyone is amazed.

Questions

1. The four friends are determined to bring their friend to Jesus. Do people or circumstances easily prevent us from coming into the presence of Christ? Can we 'believe' on behalf of others?

2. We might have expected the religious leaders to welcome Jesus, why do you think they found him so uncomfortable? Why do good people resist, often for all the best reasons, some new work of God?

3. There is often a link between a person's health and their lifestyle; can you think of examples of this?

Sickness and sin

This incident raises the difficult question of the inter-relation of sin and disease, of forgiveness and healing.

In the Old Testament these are frequently linked (e.g. 2 Chronicles 7:14; Psalm 103:3) and at times 'healing and forgiveness' are virtually interchangeable terms (e.g. Psalm 41:4; Jeremiah 3:22).

The rabbis had a saying 'There is no sick man healed of his wickedness until all his sins have been forgiven'.

Whether there was a direct connection between this man's illness and his burden of guilt we cannot tell. Modern medicine certainly recognises the value of forgiveness for general health and well-being. If the breach of a relationship with another person can cause ill-health, how much more the breakdown of our relationship with God caused by sin.

This is not to say that there is a direct relationship between personal sin and suffering. This was the repeated argument of Job's comforters whose case would simply not fit their shallow reasoning. Some sickness is undoubtedly caused by sin, our own or that of others, but there is much that is simply part and parcel of a fallen world.

The effects of mankind's fall are felt by us all, even creation itself is affected according to Paul (Romans 8:22). This world is not as God made it to be.

But, although we live in a fallen world, it is not an abandoned world. The coming of Christ marks the breaking in of the Kingdom of God with its good news of healing and forgiveness.

When the teachers of the law challenge Jesus about what he has said with their unspoken question, 'Who can forgive sins but God alone?', his response is not, 'You are mistaken, men can forgive sins too', or, 'I am not really forgiving the man just assuring him of God's forgiveness'. He accepts the correctness of their words and goes on to show just who he is and what he is able to do.

Teachers of the law

The teachers of the law or scribes, were specialists in the law and its interpretation. They were only ordained as scribes after a sustained period of study. A man would be around forty years of age before being fully qualified as a scribe.

They held many important posts in the community and were held in high regard by the people. Ordinary Jews would sit with rapt attention as they taught for the scribes knew the sacred language of Hebrew, whereas the common people only spoke Aramaic. They were given the highest places at feasts and special seats in synagogues. When they arrived at Peter's house that day the crowd would have parted to have allowed them in! They were the intellectual and religious aristocracy of the day.

They are frequently mentioned in Mark's gospel, but only once in favourable terms (12:28–34). We meet others elsewhere in the New Testament, for example Nicodemus in John 3 and Gamaliel in Acts 5. The Apostle Paul may have been a teacher of the law before his conversion.

Being experts in the law, the scribes would be responsible for passing judgment on individual cases and the personal application of the oral tradition. As far as they were concerned Jesus was clearly breaking the law claiming to speak for God. Only God could forgive sin. According to their teaching, even the Messiah could not forgive.

By his words and subsequent action Jesus was signing his own death warrant (Leviticus 24:16). The teachers of the law would have been left puzzled and angry.

Mark 2:13–17

An unlikely follower: a further controversy

Jesus chooses a man for his team who may well surprise us and certainly offended the Pharisees. Jesus had come for those who were prepared to admit their need.

 If Jesus had shown us a draft copy of the proposed twelve disciples Levi would have been the first name we would have crossed off the list. But Jesus specialises in calling and using unlikely people. Never was there a more unpromising candidate than Levi.

As often, after a miracle has taken place, Jesus withdraws from the crowd (see 1:45; 3:7, 13; 4:1; 5:21 etc.). He wants to allow the dust to settle before he makes his next move. It gave him time to recharge his spiritual resources as well as giving the people the opportunity to reflect on the deeper meaning of what was happening among them.

Mark gives us just the basic details of Levi's call – his name (this is the Matthew of Mark 3:18, see Matthew 9:9), his occupation – tax collector (see p. 47), the call and Levi's response. Tax collectors were notoriously dishonest and greatly disliked by their fellow Jews. They were considered traitors and outcasts. We may be surprised that Jesus would want someone like Levi in his team, but it is Jesus who takes the initiative. Directly and personally the call comes and Levi responds immediately. He had probably heard some of Jesus' preaching there in Capernaum, perhaps seen some of his miracles. He may even have known the fishermen who were now with Jesus. It has also been suggested that James, another one of the Twelve, might have been his brother, for he is also described as 'son of Alphaeus' (3:18).

What had gone before we cannot tell. We only know that when the call came Levi responded and surely never regretted it. There is a sense in which he had more to lose than the fishermen. If things did not work out Peter and the others could have returned to their fishing but for Levi there was no going back. He is overwhelmed by the love and acceptance of Jesus.

As a spontaneous expression of joy, Levi throws a party for all his old friends and colleagues. We can imagine every rogue in the district being there, shoulder to shoulder with Jesus. Levi wanted to honour his new-found Master and give others the chance to meet him. It was the first evangelistic dinner!

The Pharisees (see p. 48) are scandalised. Jesus is mixing with all the riff-raff of the city. They consider his conduct to be disgraceful. Jesus silences them with a traditional proverb (verse 17). It is not those who think they are alright who need help but those who know they are not. Jesus will go where the need is, like a doctor caring for the sick.

A Jewish scholar was asked, at what point, if any, the teaching of Jesus was completely new and original. He found it in this. The Jewish teachers said that if a sinner returned to God and made the right sacrifices, God would receive and forgive him. Jesus shows us a God who goes out to look for lost sinners. '... the Son of Man came to seek and to save what was lost.' (Luke 19:10)

This does not mean that the Pharisees are 'righteous' in the New Testament sense of being 'right with God' (Romans 3:19–20) nor that Jesus did not have time for good people. The sad thing was that the Pharisees did not realise that they were sinners in need of a Saviour also. Their confidence in their own righteousness made them deaf to the call to repentance. Outcasts who were aware of their need were finding their way into the Kingdom.

Questions

1. How can we as Christians mix with those with very different life styles from our own without compromising our moral standards? Are we tempted to withdraw from society for fear of contamination?

2. The Pharisees found it hard to admit their need of Jesus. How can we help 'good' people to be aware of their need?

3. Do you think Levi gave up being a tax-collector at this point? Or did he keep his profession going 'on the side', like the fishermen among the disciples? If he didn't give it up, should he have done so? Why?

Tax collectors

At the time of Jesus, Palestine was a subject nation, a part of the Roman Empire. The task of tax collecting was farmed out to the highest bidder and as long as the collector handed over the assessed figure at the end of the year, he could retain whatever else he managed to extract from his fellow Jews. Ordinary folk had no idea what they were actually supposed to pay.

Tax collectors tended to be rich and unpopular. Capernaum stood at the meeting point of several main roads and marked the border of Herod Antipas' territory. As a busy customs post it would have had many tax collectors and there were rich pickings to be had.

There were two types of tax to be paid. Statutory taxes that included income tax and ground tax, and a very fluid kind of duty that was payable on any number of things. This was payable for using main roads, harbours, markets, bridges etc.

A man could be charged not only for his cart but for each wheel of it and the animal that pulled it. A tax collector could stop a traveller on the road, order him to unpack his belongings and charge him well nigh what he liked. Sometimes they would charge impossibly high sums, then lend the money at a very high rate of interest.

Tax collectors were generally dishonest (see Luke 3:12–13; 19:1–10). In fact, in some towns statues were erected to honest tax collectors – they were so rare! They were not paid a salary as such, their only income was commission. It was difficult, therefore, for an honest man to survive in the business. Not only were they looked upon as thieves, but also as traitors, exploiting their fellow countrymen. In the Jewish Talmud (an ancient collection of Jewish writings) tax collectors were linked with 'murderers and robbers'. Also their contact with the Gentile Romans made them ritually unclean. They were not allowed to enter the synagogue or give evidence in court. They were considered as unclean as a leprosy sufferer.

In Capernaum, like Zacchaeus in Jericho, Levi would have been the man everybody hated. But Jesus chose Levi!

Pharisees

This is the first time in Mark's gospel that we meet the Pharisees. They first appear in Jewish history during the time between the Old and the New Testaments, as a sincere and dedicated reform group within Israel. They were deeply devoted to the law and its careful observance. By the time of Jesus they were the most influential religious party.

Their name means 'separated' and separation was at the heart of their understanding of what it meant to please God.

They stood for the distinctiveness of Israel as God's chosen people and the need for the holy people of God to be different. Unfortunately, this degenerated into a religious exclusivism. They forgot Israel's destiny to be a light for the Gentiles (Isaiah 42:6; 49:6) and withdrew from all contact with heathen people.

They became aloof and superior, scornful not only of Gentiles but also of ordinary Jews who did not practice the same kind of separation as themselves. The phrase '"sinners" and tax collectors' (verse 16) probably originated with them. Tax collectors were notorious for being in the employment of pagan Rome. 'Sinners' was their umbrella term for everyone who failed to observe their rules and traditions. Sadly, the Pharisees had no time for such people.

The Pharisees were not always popular but they were respected for their dedication. Most of them were sincere in their desire to do the right thing, but their principal concern was their own purity rather than the needs of others. It was inevitable that Jesus' approach would fall foul of them. 'This man welcomes sinners, and eats with them' they complained (Luke 15:2). What they intended as a criticism, Christians rejoice in as being a truth that is at the heart of the gospel.

Mark 2:18-22

When Jesus won't fit in

Jesus is taken to task by the Pharisees for apparently disregarding accepted religious practices. He helps us to understand and appreciate that there is a new way.

This is round three in the contest between Jesus and the religious leaders of the day. They were offended by the claims he made, the company he kept and now by the customs he seems to disregard.

To fast is to abstain from food for spiritual purposes and it is a practice common to many religions. By the time of Jesus it had developed into a compulsory and complicated ritual. The Old Testament itself instructed fasting to take place on just one day each year – the all-important Day of Atonement. It was to be an expression of repentance before the sacrifices for sin were made. But as time went on traditions grew, customs developed and by this time the Pharisees were fasting twice a week (every Monday and Thursday, which just happened to be market days in Jerusalem!). What was intended to be a quiet and humble religious discipline had become an elaborate act of religious showmanship and spiritual pride.

Jesus maintained that fasting was inappropriate just now. He had come to bring something totally and wonderfully new. To try to squeeze the new life-giving wine of the Kingdom into the stiff old wineskins of Jewish legalism would lead to disaster. New wineskins were flexible and would give as the new wine continued to ferment. The days of patching up old things are over. The new message Jesus came to bring could not be poured into the old mould. Jesus had come to turn water into wine (John 2:1–11).

Jesus uses a wedding as an illustration of his coming. Weddings were very special occasions in Bible days, with celebrations some-times lasting as long as a week. The bride and groom would not go away on a honeymoon as in modern Western culture, but would keep open house for a period of continued feasting and celebration. A wedding was an oasis of joy in the middle of the dull routine of life. Guests had time off from their work and were excused all religious duties while the festivities continued. People did not fast at weddings!

Jesus coming into the world was an outburst of joy. God's Messiah, the heavenly bridegroom, was here. Fasting, an expression of sorrow, was totally out of place. This was a time for feasting not fasting. But, Jesus indicates there will be a time for fasting later, when he is 'taken' from them. The expression is a violent one, used twice in Isaiah 53:8. 'By oppression and judgment he was *taken away*. And who can speak of his descendants? For he was *cut off* from the land of the living; for the transgressions of my people he was stricken.' The long shadow of the cross stretches across Mark's gospel. Jesus knew that he would have to die and that this would be a time of sadness for his followers. It would be right for them to fast then.

In the Sermon on the Mount Jesus gives teaching on fasting alongside giving and praying, assuming that his disciples will do all three (Matthew 6:1–18).

As the church awaits the return of the Heavenly Bridegroom, many Christians would testify to the continuing value of fasting as an optional personal discipline. 'It was not Christ's intention to reject or despise fasting' said Martin Luther, 'It was his intention to restore proper fasting.'

Questions

1. How would you summarise Jesus' attitude to fasting? Does he for-bid it or command it? (cf. Matthew 6:16–18; Mark 9:29)

2. What would you feel is the value of fasting? What are its potential dangers?

3. The Pharisees were finding that the new life of the Kingdom would not fit their own man-made traditions. Is the church in danger today of trying to restrict the way God works to its own struc-tures and traditions? How can we avoid this?

Mark 2:23 – 3:6

People matter more than rules

The initial conflict with the Pharisees reaches its climax. The issue this time is Sabbath observance. The section ends with the first plot to kill Jesus.

In this passage Jesus steps out of line in two ways as far as the Pharisees were concerned. Firstly, he allows his disciples to pluck ears of corn on the Sabbath, and then he heals a man with a damaged hand, again on the Sabbath.

What the disciples were doing was perfectly permissible under Jewish law (Deuteronomy 23:25). It was not stealing. The issue was not what they were doing but *when* they were doing it. To pluck ears of corn would be considered reaping, that is, working. And working was forbidden on the Sabbath.

Jesus answers with an appeal to Scripture. The incident is recorded in 1 Samuel 21:1–6. The consecrated bread was especially dedicated to God and could only be used in the service of the Temple. Only the priests were allowed to eat it. But David, one of the heroes of Jewish history, disregarded this legal injunction because of the needs of his men. In other words, human needs must take priority over ritual laws. People come first.

The same truth is illustrated in the incident that follows. Jewish law said that if a man transgressed once he should be warned; if he went wrong a second time he was to be punished. This has led some to suggest that the man with a damaged hand was a plant by the Pharisees to trap Jesus.

Breaking of the Sabbath laws was punishable by death (see Exodus 31:14–17 and an example of this in Numbers 15). The Pharisees' rule was that as long as there was no actual danger to life healing should be postponed until the next day.

In none of the seven occasions recorded in the gospels that Jesus heals on the Sabbath would the Pharisees have said that there was an immediate danger of death (e.g. Luke 13:10–14). Certainly this man seems to have had a long-standing problem.

Verse four gives us one of Jesus' unanswerable questions. To refuse to do good on the Sabbath was surely to choose to do evil. It seems that the Pharisees have no doubt about Jesus' ability to perform the healing.

Jesus is both angry and sad. Angry at the insensitivity and callousness. Sad that they could not see beyond their rigid legal framework. After the man is healed, no-one comments or praises God. The Pharisees stalk off in protest and begin to make plans with a group whom they normally had nothing to do with, the Herodians. This negative alliance is destined to continue (12:13). The rift between Jesus and the religious leaders is greater than ever.

Questions

1. Jesus tells us that the Sabbath is a gift from God – how should we use this gift constructively? How can we keep one day special for God without making the same mistakes as the Pharisees? Could you defend the way you spend Sunday before the Lord?

2. Have we, as Christians, any right to tell others what they can or cannot do on a Sunday? What about Sunday trading?

3. The Pharisees looked closely and critically at the activities of Jesus and his disciples. How can Jesus' responses be a model for us when challenged?

 ## Sabbath observance

The observance of the seventh day as a day of rest is a part of God's provision for mankind in creation. It was a gift from God for our benefit. The Pharisees had so complicated the day with their rules and regulations that they had destroyed its very character. What God had intended as a blessing had been turned into a wearisome burden.

For example, it was forbidden to wear heavy shoes on the Sabbath. Otherwise, each time you lifted your foot you would be guilty of carrying a burden! Looking in the mirror was forbidden, you might see a grey hair and be tempted to pull it out and that would be working on the Sabbath! It was even forbidden to eat an egg that had been laid on the Sabbath for that would be encouraging hens to break the fourth commandment! The laws were petty and complex.

There were thirty-nine broad classes of forbidden work with endless subdivisions and qualifications. Finger nails were not to be cut; only one letter was to be written; a bucket could be tied to a belt but not a rope. Every conceivable circumstance was covered: what sort of knots could be tied; how far anything could be thrown; where on a person anything could be carried; how far you could walk etc. The Jewish Mishnah itself comments, 'The rules about the Sabbath are as a mountain hanging by a hair, for the scripture is scanty and the rules are many'.

Jesus wanted to restore a true perspective and appreciation of God's special day. Attempts to abandon it have always proved disastrous. For example, just after the French Revolution there was an attempt to bring in a ten-day week! During the Second World War, some companies tried to work a seven-day week to step up production. *The News Review* of 28 May 1942 wrote, 'A seven day week for industry yields decreased production, increased accidents and intensified absenteeism.'

People are geared to a seven-day week, with one day as a rest day. It is part of the Maker's plan – a creation ordinance, as theologians call it. The traditional Jewish Sabbath provides the basis for our distinctively Christian Sabbath, the Lord's Day. Christians should value it as a precious gift from God.

4

VARIOUS REACTIONS
Mark 3:7–35

Jesus' ministry demands a response. Time and again Jesus goes to the heart of the issue and presents a clear choice to both his followers and opponents. Jesus does not flinch from this opposition even when it comes, most painfully, from family and friends.

Mark 3:7–19

Jesus chooses his first team

In contrast to the rejection of the religious leaders, Jesus is welcomed by the ordinary people of Galilee and elsewhere. From them he chooses twelve disciples.

A new phase of Jesus' ministry is under way, that takes us through to chapter six. It begins with the calling of the disciples and ends with them being sent out on their mission (6:6–13). Like George Whitefield and John and Charles Wesley were to do many years later, Jesus turns from the religious establishments of the day to take his message out into the open air.

We should see this as a strategic withdrawal. It was not time for the final conflict yet, others needed to hear and those who were going to continue his ministry needed to be appointed. Jesus' popularity is a marked contrast to the opposition he has met in the synagogue from the religious leaders. People come from many miles around and in large numbers.

The places mentioned in verse 8 make up a comprehensive list of Israel and her immediate neighbours (see map on p. 14). Galilee, Judea and Jerusalem are part of Israel; Idumea, Transjordan, Tyre and Sidon mark the southern, eastern and northern borders. They will have travelled on foot for many miles. Jerusalem, for example, was some one hundred miles away. It is a powerful indication of the popularity of Jesus.

But, we must ask, why had they come? Sadly, it seems for the wrong reason. They had 'heard all he was doing' (verse 8). They were fascinated and impressed by Jesus' miracles. They came for healing, seeing Jesus merely as a miracle worker. They did not really understand who Jesus was or the true nature of his mission. Their response remained inadequate.

Ironically, it was only the evil spirits who really grasped who Jesus was and Jesus did not want testimony from them. This was not the time for such an open statement and they were certainly not the right messengers. Jesus had others in mind for this task – the apostles.

Mark tells us that Jesus chose twelve disciples (see p. 58) to be with him and to be sent out from him. The call of Jesus has the note of a summons about it.

Several things strike us about the Twelve. Firstly, how ordinary they were. There is not a priest or scribe or Pharisee among them. They have no special qualifications, no real academic achievements, social position or wealth. We might describe them as twelve every-day working men. Peter and John are described in Acts 4:13 as 'unschooled, ordinary men'.

Secondly, we note what a mixed bag they were. There is the impetuous Simon Peter, the ambitious James and John, the shy Andrew, the unemotional Philip, the conservative Bartholomew, the former tax collector Matthew, the melancholy Thomas, the hidden James, son of Alphaeus and Thaddeus, the radical Simon the Zealot and Judas Iscariot. William Barclay comments, 'The plain fact is that if Simon the Zealot had met Matthew anywhere else than in the company of Jesus, he would have stuck a dagger in him'.

In spite of their differences in temperament, in background and personality, these were the ones Jesus wanted.

He chose them, we are told, for two purposes – to be his companions and to be his representatives. The first thing Jesus offered them was friendship, in spite of his relationship with the Father Jesus wanted human companionship. Then, they were to be 'sent out' to preach. The word used is a violent one, used for throwing out the rubbish! They are to be thrust out. The task of taking the good news is so important and urgent but Jesus' followers are often so reluctant that they need a good push to get them going!

Questions

1. Jesus' call to his disciples was twofold – to be with him and to be sent out from him. Some Christians would like to spend all their time 'with Jesus', others feel the task is so urgent there is no time to 'waste' in fellowship and worship. Does your church get the balance right?

2. Jesus chose a real variety of people for his team; which disciple do you feel that you are most like? In what way can Jesus use our natural characteristics in his service?

3. Why do you think Jesus did not choose women as part of his team?

The 'Twelve'

The 'Twelve' is a distinctive way that Mark has of describing the group of disciples. He uses the term ten times, whereas Matthew and Luke only use it six times each and John only four times. We are clearly meant to see a parallel between the twelve disciples and the twelve tribes of Israel. They represent the beginning of a new 'Israel', the church (see Matthew 19:28).

The names of the Twelve are listed in four places in the New Testament: Matthew 10:2–4; Luke 6:14–16; Acts 1:13 and here in Mark 3:16–19. The Thaddeus in Mark is probably the Judas, son of James, in Acts, for it was not uncommon for a man to have up to three names (see Acts 1:23 for an example). Again, the Bartholomew of Mark is probably the Nathaniel of John's gospel, for Bartholomew never appears in the fourth gospel and Nathaniel never appears in Matthew, Mark or Luke. Bartholomew would have been a second name meaning son of Tolmai. In the first three gospels Bartholomew is generally linked with Philip whereas in John's gospel Nathaniel is connected with Philip. There is every reason for believing that Bartholomew and Nathaniel are the same person.

Simon heads each list and was clearly a leader among the disciples. He is given a new name by Jesus, Cephas or Peter, which means 'rock'. John tells us in his gospel how Jesus saw the potential in this unpredictable man. 'You are Simon, son of John. You will be called Cephas.' (John 1:42) Jesus sees us as we are, but also as we could be.

James and John are given the name 'Boanerges', reflecting their sudden bursts of temper (e.g. see Luke 9:51–56). Their ambition comes through in Mark 10:35f, and their intolerance in Mark 9:38. Andrew is listed next as the last of the first four (1:16). The names which follow, with the exception of Judas Iscariot, do not occur again in Mark's account.

Mark 3:20–35

Misunderstood and misrepresented

In this passage, we see two groups of people coming to mistaken conclusions about Jesus. One is born of concern, the other of malice.

Jesus is under fire in these dramatic verses. As the first phase of Jesus' ministry is drawing to a close, people are beginning to form opinions about him. Where does his power come from? How he is able to do the things he does? A person cannot be close to Jesus for long without having to come to some sort of verdict about him.

Mark begins by telling us about Jesus' family (verses 21–22; see p. 61), an incident that is not recorded by any of the other gospel writers. The narrative is interrupted by the accusation of the teachers of the law and then returns to the concerns of Jesus' family (verse 31). The setting is probably Simon Peter's home in Capernaum and we sense the kind of pressure Jesus often lived under, leaving no time for a meal. Members of his family arrive from Nazareth some twenty miles away. They had heard worrying reports that people were saying that Jesus was mad. Whether they shared this impression is unclear. The 'they' of verse 21 could mean 'people were saying ... ' or 'they, his family were saying ... ' If the latter is the case we can imagine how painful this must have been for Jesus. To be misrepresented by his opponents was one thing but to be misunderstood by those close to him would have been much harder to bear.

We find it hard to think why anyone should think that Jesus was insane. It was surely not the things he said or did that brought people to this misguided suggestion. His words were full of authority, leaving people amazed and his actions breathed love and compassion.

The most likely explanation is that it was his sheer dedication that brought this accusation. Some perhaps considered it fanaticism – missing meals in order to help people, taking a path that would inevitably lead to confrontation with the religious authorities, choosing twelve such non-starters as his disciples. He must be crazy, they said, to throw aside both security and safety in this way. If the 'family' shared this view it was surely out of genuine concern for him, so they come to 'take charge' of him. The word Mark uses can mean 'to arrest' someone. They are worried for his safety and sanity so seek to bring him home. It was a well-meaning but mistaken action.

The accusation of the Pharisees is of a very different kind. Jesus' fame has spread and an official deputation from Jerusalem arrives to investigate what is going on. They cannot deny the reality of his miracles so they attack his motivation. 'He has power over demons because he is in partnership with the devil'. It was a ridiculous suggestion. Jesus demonstrates its absurdity with two little parables. First of all, says Jesus, if I'm casting out demons by the power of Satan, then it's like a dog biting it's own tail. The forces of evil are destroying themselves. A divided kingdom will not last long. But not only is Jesus opposed to Satan, he is also stronger than Satan. Before a gang of burglars can steal the goods from a house they must tie up the owner. Then they can take what they like.

Although Satan is strong and holds people in his grip, now Jesus has bound him so that people can be set free (1 John 3:8).

It seems that the scribes were concerned for their own reputation and were jealous of Jesus' success and popularity. Their prejudice prompts Jesus to make one of his most solemn statements in the gospel. Its seriousness is underlined by the introductory phrase 'I tell you the truth'. This expression is found many times in the gospels and Jesus uses it when he has something of particular importance to say.

It is vital to read Jesus' words in their context. He is saying that what these critics are doing, namely ascribing the work of God's Spirit to the power of Satan, is to commit a sin that will not be forgiven (see p. 62). What greater blasphemy could there be than to deliberately reject the wonderful things Jesus was doing and attribute them to the devil?

Mark returns to the reaction of the family. Here and in 6:3 are the only two places where Mary, Jesus' mother, is referred to by name. Jesus is not, of course, denying the responsibility a Christian should have for his family; the New Testament is consistent on the importance of family ties (e.g. Mark 7:9–13; 1 Timothy 5:8) but he is saying that there are ties that are even stronger now. The Kingdom 'family' is a family to which all who obey God belong. These new ties are deeper even than flesh and blood.

Questions

1. If Jesus' family shared the view that Jesus was out of his mind, what might have driven them to this idea? Have you ever been misunderstood or rejected by those closest to you because of your commitment to Christ?

2. The words about Jesus' family seem to imply a criticism of the family unit (see verses 33–35); do you find Jesus' words surprising? How do we reconcile Jesus' response with the command to honour father and mother? (Exodus 20:12)

3. What do you understand by 'whoever blasphemes against the Holy Spirit' (verse 29)? How would you counsel someone who felt they had been guilty of this? Is 'blasphemy against the Holy Spirit' the same as 'grieving the Holy Spirit' (Ephesians 4:30)? What is the difference, if any?

Jesus' family

Exact details of Jesus' family are limited. Much discussion has revolved around the question as to whether Mark has 'cousins' or children of Joseph by a former marriage in mind. But the most natural understanding of these verses is that these were natural brothers of Jesus and that he was the eldest in the family. The absence of any reference to Joseph has given rise to the widely held view that he had died by this time.

The brothers seem largely unimpressed with Jesus during his earthly ministry but we do know that his brother James became a Christian after the death and resurrection of Jesus (1 Corinthians 15:7). He was an important leader in the Jerusalem church.

For Jesus, obedience to the will of God was fundamental in the Kingdom of God. He is not belittling family ties in these verses but underlying the importance of a wider fellowship that transcends natural ties. Even as basic a relationship as that of a human family is superseded by the new family of the Kingdom (Mark 10:28–30).

It has been suggested that the 'family' of verse 21 is not the 'mother and brothers' of verse 31, but wider family relations. Could it be that the extended family were putting pressure on Mary and her sons? The prominence Jesus was enjoying was clearly attracting the attention of the authorities. Others had been this way before and it had ended in arrest, imprisonment and death. We can understand family affection overriding clearer judgment.

An unforgivable sin?

Many Christians have been troubled or confused about Jesus' words about blasphemy against the Holy Spirit. It seems very strange to hear him speak of a sin for which there is no forgiveness. What does he mean?

It is perhaps easier to begin by saying what the unforgivable sin is *not*. Certainly it is not an exhausting of the love and patience of God. It is not God saying 'I've had enough of that person, they have sinned once too often'. This would be against the whole tenor of Scripture (e.g. Isaiah 1:18; Jeremiah 31:3; 1 John 1:7, 9).

Again, it is not a particularly serious sin. Some early Christian writers classified sins into forgivable and unforgivable. Tertullian (AD 160–215), for example, listed murder, adultery, blasphemy and idolatry as beyond forgiveness. From this the idea of seven deadly sins grew up. This is clearly not a biblical idea. We only have to consider some of the sins of the characters of Scripture who received forgiveness. For example the adultery and murder committed by David, the persecution of Christians at the hand of Saul. Paul gives a list of sins in 1 Corinthians 6:9–10, including such things as sexual immorality, adultery, homosexual acts, and we wonder 'Is any one of these the unpardonable sin?' No, for Paul continues 'And that is what some of you were. But you were washed, you were sanctified, you were justified in the name of the Lord Jesus Christ and by the Spirit of our God.' (1 Corinthians 6:11) The grace of God is big enough to cover any and every sin.

What then does Jesus have in mind? It is surely the attitude demonstrated here by the teachers of the law. They attribute the works and words of Jesus to the evil one. They wilfully reject the truth as he stands before them. The unforgivable sin is a deliberate and knowing rejection of Christ. It is not an isolated act but a wilful attitude. It is not a sin that can be committed accidentally or unknowingly. Indeed a concern over sin is the very opposite to the attitude in question here. It is rather an indifference to sin, a cynical rejection of the grace of God. It is not a sin a Christian can commit.

The unpardonable sin therefore, is to have a clear knowledge of the way of forgiveness but to deliberately reject it. Such a sin cannot by definition be forgiven.

We can trace a hardening in the attitude of the religious leaders to Jesus in these early chapters of Mark's gospel. In 2:7 they accuse Jesus of blasphemy; in 3:6 they plan to kill him and now in 3:22 they attribute his work to the devil. They have 'written off' Jesus Christ and, therefore, denied themselves the possibility of forgiveness. Again, we note, Jesus is warning them against it, not saying they have committed it.

5

PARABLES OF
THE KINGDOM
Mark 4:1–41

Mark has shown us Jesus 'in action', now he illustrates one of the
key features of Jesus' teaching method – parables. Jesus' parables
are spiritual time bombs. On the surface they seem like harmless
stories, but suddenly they explode with powerful meaning.

Mark 4:1–20

Truth in a story

Jesus compares the spreading of the gospel to the sowing of seed. Although some seed may be lost, there will be a bumper harvest.

One of the most familiar characteristics of Jesus' teaching ministry was his use of parables (see p. 68). He was not the first to use this method, there are parables in the Old Testament (e.g. 2 Samuel 12:1–7; Isaiah 5:1–7) and Jewish rabbis of the day used them, but Jesus' parables have a power that is all their own. It was his favourite teaching method, putting truth in a simple, thought-provoking and memorable form. Many people who know little of Jesus and his claims know about the Good Samaritan, the Prodigal Son and the Sower.

Jesus was faced with a problem similar to that which often confronts the church today – how do you reach people with closed minds? How do you make people with preconceived ideas about God and life examine these preconceptions and ask deeper questions? A parable would awake new interest, stimulate fresh thought and force people to examine old ideas. Jesus' parables are spiritual time bombs. On the surface, they seemed like harmless stories, but in time they explode with powerful meaning. One of P.G. Wodehouse's characters complains, 'A parable is one of those stories in the Bible which sound at first like a pleasant yarn, but keeps something up its sleeve which suddenly pops up and knocks you flat.' They almost inevitably contain this element of surprise and a listener is left thinking, 'I never thought of it like that before'.

The parable of the sower is the first that Mark records and it is found in all three synoptic (Matthew, Mark, Luke) gospels. It is a key parable (verse 13). It reflects farming practice in Palestine where ploughing followed sowing. Unlike many countries today where the soil is prepared before the planting takes place, the seed would be scattered widely and then ploughed in. This is not the parable of the Careless Gardener! The path for example, was not a concrete pathway but simply a route that had been trodden down by passers-by. The seed on the thin topsoil would also have been sown intentionally, for the underlying limestone would not show until the ploughing revealed it. The seed that fell amongst the weeds would also be ploughed in.

This is not wastefulness or inefficiency on behalf of the sower, but it is an illustration of the grace of God. God's message, God's seed is for all, but not everyone will receive it. It is not the sower or the seed that is the problem but the soil. That is why this parable is sometimes called 'The parable of the soils'.

Jesus illustrates four responses to his word.

- Firstly, a superficial response that is really no response at all (verses 4 and 15). The seed does not penetrate and is quickly lost. We think of the vast crowds that were attracted to Jesus but were soon to slip away.

- Secondly, a shallow response from the rocky soil (verses 5 and 6; 16 and 17). This is not soil that is filled with stones, but a thin layer of soil, perhaps only a few centimetres, that rests on limestone rock. This is very common in Palestine. The seed would germinate quickly but because there was no depth of soil, as soon as the roots began to search for moisture they would meet only rock and the plant would shrivel up in the heat and die.

  Many who initially began to follow Jesus quickly turned away when he began to speak about the cost of discipleship.

- Thirdly, a shared response (verses 7, 18 and 19), where the seed is welcomed but so is everything else! God's word is crowded out by the weeds of anxiety or the thorns of success. Slowly, subtly, but just as effectively, the seed is destroyed. Demas (2 Timothy 4:10) remains a sad New Testament example of this.

- But, says Jesus, there is a satisfactory response. There is some soil that is soft, deep and clean, where the seed is received, nourished and grows. Experts say that tenfold is an average harvest, thirty-fold is good, sixtyfold is excellent, one hundredfold is amazing! In spite of the hazards and losses the sower enjoys a splendid harvest.

It all depends on how we listen to God's word.

Questions

1. Why do you think Jesus used parables rather than making simple statements of truth? What does this have to teach us in the way we seek to communicate the gospel today?

2. Have you ever taken a non-Christian friend to hear the gospel and been disappointed at their lack of response? Is there encouragement for you here in this parable? Should we expect three out of four converts to lose their way?

3. Can *churches* be like these different types of seed and soil – or is Jesus just thinking of individual disciples?

4. Do verses 10–12 imply that God deliberately obscures revelation from people? What do you think Jesus meant by 'the secret of the Kingdom of God'?

 ## Jesus' use of parables

A parable is an extended metaphor (figure of speech) or simile (likening one thing to another). We use them all the time, for example, the garden is like a jungle, the children behaved like animals. They were very common in Bible days.

Indeed, the Old Testament book we know as 'Proverbs' could be called 'Parables', for it is the same Hebrew word. The root meaning of the word is to put things side by side, that is, to make a comparison. The word is only used twice in the New Testament outside the gospels (Hebrews 9:9; 11:19).

The essential reason why Jesus used parables was in order to communicate. He was able to express profound truths in simple, down-to-earth stories. His parables would have created interest and were probably produced on the spur of the moment. (Perhaps Jesus saw a sower across the hillside and this prompted the story.)

Parables are truth in picture form. How could ordinary Galilean folk grasp an abstract concept like the Kingdom of God? Jesus paints pictures in words for them and for us. The Kingdom of God is like a seed ... a wedding feast ... a treasure, etc. The teaching would be much more readily understood and remembered, for Jesus' teaching was spoken not written down.

Jesus used parables to communicate truth in a way that was accessible, powerful and memorable. But what are we to make of his words in verses 10–12 that seem to contradict this?

Several attempts have been made to 'soften' Jesus' words. There are some who suggest these words do not go back to Jesus at all but are a later formulation by the church designed to explain why people are not responding to the gospel.

Others suggest the phrase 'so that' in verse 12 should read 'as a result'. In other words that this is not the purpose of Jesus' parables but merely the outcome.

It is important to note that these difficult words are spoken to the disciples and not the crowd. Jesus is responding to the question, 'Why do the crowds get a parable but the disciples are given plain teaching?' Jesus sees a clear distinction between the crowd and the disciples.

There is throughout the gospel a subtlety about Jesus' approach. He will always reveal enough of God's truth for faith to make its response. Where there is a response then more truth can be given. A parable would sort out those who were keen to listen and learn from those who were just casual in their interest. For them a parable would have the challenge to respond and the warning of judgment if they failed to do so.

The truth is there for those who have eyes to see it but Jesus will not compel belief or waste further revelation on those who have not responded to the truth they have already been given.

The 'secret' of the Kingdom

Mark uses a technical term here, translated either as 'secret' or 'mystery'. It is a favourite word of Paul's. He uses it twenty-one times in his letters (e.g. Ephesians 1:9; Colossians 1:27). It does not refer to something mysterious, like a modern detective story, or hidden. Rather, it refers to something previously unknown that has now been revealed. So Paul can refer to the gospel as a 'mystery hidden for long ages past' (Romans 16:25).

The New Testament use of the word stands in direct contrast to ancient mystery religions. Pagan religions protected their mysterious truths from ordinary folk. Only after a long period of preparation and initiation was a person allowed in on the secret. But God's 'mystery' is not a closely guarded secret but an open revelation for all who will receive it.

Although the mystery is beyond human discovery it has now been revealed by God. For Mark the secret of the Kingdom is Jesus. The disciples are beginning to recognise who Jesus is and therefore beginning to understand the mystery. It was not immediately obvious to many that the Kingdom had come in Jesus. They were expecting a very different kind of Messiah.

Mark 4:21–34

How God's word works

The good news that Jesus has brought is not to be kept to ourselves; it is to be shared with others. As we plant the seed of the gospel in people's lives we can expect a harvest.

 The River Jordan supplies two large lakes. One, the Sea of Galilee, is full of fish and plant life. The other, the Dead Sea, has nothing living in it at all. It is stagnant and lifeless. Both lakes have the same source but only the Sea of Galilee has an outlet. In other words, it passes on what it has received, whereas the Dead Sea does not. That is the challenge of the parables in this passage, the message that Jesus has brought is not to be kept to ourselves but it is to be passed on to others.

It would be foolish to light a lamp and then put it under a bowl or a bed when its purpose is to illuminate the whole room (verse 21). The message of Jesus' coming is not to be hidden away but shared as widely as possible (verse 22). Only as the disciples share the light they have received will they be able to receive more light from their Lord (verses 24–25).

But how will people respond to their message? The indications are that many will be indifferent or hostile like the unresponsive soils in the parable of the sower. Jesus tells them two further parables to encourage them (and us) that although the going may be tough at times there will be an exciting harvest.

The parable of the seed growing secretly (verses 26–29) is unique to Mark's gospel. It tells us a number of things about the growth of God's word in people's lives.

- Firstly, the seed's growth is mysterious (verse 27). The miracle of growth is hidden from us. Imperceptibly the seed begins to grow, just as God's Spirit blows freely like the wind (John 3:8).

71

Sharing the gospel is never just a matter of formulas and techniques, there will always be this extra dimension, the mysterious working of God.

- Secondly, the growth of the seed is gradual (verse 28). The sower needs patience. We cannot plant today and pick the fruit tomorrow! The seed needs time to germinate and grow (cf. James 5:7–8). Jesus is drawing parallels between the way things are in nature and how they are in the Kingdom of God.

- Thirdly, the seed's growth is certain (cf. 1 Corinthians 3:7). It is interesting to notice in how few words the farmer's work is described. While the man sleeps, the seed grows, 'all by itself ...' (verse 28). The only other time this word is used in the New Testament is in Acts 12:10 when the prison gate opens 'by itself', automatically, to let Peter go free. The seed's growth is inherent in the seed. When it is faithfully sown it will grow (cf. Romans 1:16), and there will be a harvest.

The last parable in this section underlines this. From the tiny mustard seed a large plant grows. From insignificant beginnings a great movement develops. The disciples might easily have felt discouraged when they thought of the vastness of their task – how could twelve weak, ordinary people hope to reach the world? The mustard seed was proverbial in Jewish thinking as the smallest of seeds, yet it could grow into a tree some two metres high.

The reference to the 'birds of the air' perching in its shade is possibly a reference to the Gentiles finding their place in the Kingdom. Birds liked to eat the little black seeds of a mustard tree and would often gather in its branches.

When God begins something there is no telling where it will end! (cf. Revelation 5:9) The disciples should not be put off by the outward appearance of things or the apparent lack of response. There is no doubt in Jesus' mind that when the seed is sown a process begins that will bear fruit in God's time.

Mark indicates (verse 33) that he is only giving us a selection of Jesus' parables and tells us the principle that Jesus operated by. We see an example of this in John 16:12. Jesus was fully aware of the capacity of his listeners. He reserved detailed explanations for the disciples, parables gave the crowd time to think and prevented them coming to premature and probably mistaken conclusions about who he was and what he had come to do.

Questions

1. We are often tempted to hide the light of God's truth rather than let it shine. Why is this? How can we be conspicuous without becoming obnoxious?

2. On the surface, Jesus' words in verse 25 seem unfair; do you think they are? Can you think of other areas of life where this same principle applies?

3. The parables in verses 26–32 are full of encouragement. Go through them again drawing out the parts you find helpful concerning sharing your faith.

Mark 4:35–41

Jesus sleeps: the disciples panic!

In this passage Jesus demonstrates his power over nature and challenges his disciples to trust him even in the most perilous situation.

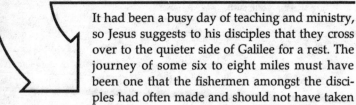 It had been a busy day of teaching and ministry, so Jesus suggests to his disciples that they cross over to the quieter side of Galilee for a rest. The journey of some six to eight miles must have been one that the fishermen amongst the disciples had often made and should not have taken long. Some 600 feet below sea level, the Sea of Galilee lies like a basin between high mountains. The cold west wind is often channelled through the valleys and gulleys and in no time at all the quiet tranquil waters can be whipped up into a frenzy. Sudden violent storms are common and evening storms, coinciding with the fall of darkness, are particularly dangerous.

The disciples were, no doubt, anticipating a gentle crossing and a welcome rest on the other side, after all it was Jesus' idea! Mark's reference to 'other boats' (verse 36) is an interesting eye-witness detail. They too would have experienced the sudden storm and the equally sudden stillness but they would not have known why. We are often caught up in the wider purposes of God that are much bigger than our own situation and whose purpose is hidden from us.

The violence of the storm is captured by Matthew's use of the word *seismos* (Matthew 8:24): it was like an earthquake. We can sense the waves and smell the fear as the waters crash over the boat. We can imagine the disciples shouting above the sound of the water, some bailing out water with whatever they could find, others battling with the oars. As the wind howls, the boat creaks, the disciples panic – Jesus sleeps!

This is the only reference we have in the gospels to Jesus being asleep. Again, in another eye-witness detail, Mark tells us that he rests his head on the helmsman's cushion. Why is he asleep? The simplest answer is that he was exhausted. Yes, this was the sleep of faith but also of genuine weariness and fatigue. This incident illustrates both the real humanity of Jesus and his powerful divinity. He is both fully man (asleep in the boat) and fully God (calming the storm). Just like you or I he is overcome with tiredness, even as he knew hunger, thirst and pain. He experienced the storms of life and is able to draw alongside us (Hebrews 4:15).

In a state of panic (this must have been quite a storm for experienced fishermen to be so afraid) the disciples wake Jesus. Their words are short and sharp. 'Don't you care?' Sometimes it seems that way. 'Why won't God do something?' With a word Jesus calms the storm: 'Quiet! Be still!' It is the same command he gives to the evil spirit in Mark 1:25. It is an authoritative order meaning literally 'Be muzzled!' The effect is immediate as the storm is stilled (see Psalm 89:8–9; 107:28–29).

The disciples are awe-struck. Before they were 'afraid': now they are 'terrified'! (verse 41) Their fear of the storm has been replaced by a new sense of wonder about the person in the boat with them. 'Who is this?', they ask. They have seen his authority over disease and demons, now they are amazed at his power over nature. The disciples are learning more about Jesus (Proverbs 9:10). Jesus wanted his disciples to be able to trust him even when he was 'asleep' and even at the heart of the storm. His presence should have been enough.

Questions

1. Imagine you are in one of the 'other boats' there that day. Describe your feelings. Can you think of times when you have been caught up in the wider purposes of God in a way that you were not aware of at the time?

2. The will of God is not always a storm-free path. Do we expect it to be so? How do we respond when it isn't? (cf. 1:12)

3. Are there times when Jesus seems to be 'asleep' just when you need him most? What help does this incident give for such times?

ACTS OF POWER
Mark 5:1 – 6:6

Mark records a further series of amazing incidents from the ministry of Jesus. We see him powerfully meeting the needs of people in the most desperate of situations. Is there no limit to what he can do? Yes there is, as the events in Nazareth demonstrate.

Mark 5:1–20

People matter more than pigs

When Jesus comes there is a wonderful new hope of freedom for the oppressed, but for some the price is too great.

What a day it had been and it wasn't over yet. Exhausted from a demanding period of teaching and healing, Jesus and his disciples decide to go by boat over to the quieter side of Galilee for a rest. A journey that should only have taken a couple of hours is disrupted by a sudden violent storm and it is perhaps the early hours of the next morning when they pull up on shore to face a 'storm' of a very different but not unrelated kind.

We have seen Jesus' authority over disease and nature, now we see it demonstrated over demons.

The exact location of this incident is unsure, but the presence of the pigs points to a predominantly Gentile area. Suddenly a frightening scream comes from the caves in the hillside that were used as tombs. No Jew would go near them for fear of being made religiously unclean through close contact with the dead. Out of the caves comes a terrifying figure. A man so dangerous that he has been held by chains, but so strong that he has broken free on many occasions. The frightened townspeople had driven him out to live among the dead. In his loneliness and isolation he mutilates himself. We can imagine the rush of fear the disciples feel as this alarming figure approaches them. The man is demon-possessed.

Jesus deals with the situation quickly and effectively. He has indisputable authority over the evil spirits that had so taken over this man's personality. The demons immediately recognise who Jesus is. When asked his name, the possessed man describes himself as Legion (in ancient Rome a regiment of three to six thousand soldiers).

The title graphically describes his condition. A conversation takes place between Jesus, the Son of God, and the army of intruders that have such a powerful grip on this man. The spirits recognise the superior power of Jesus and plead to be allowed to go into a nearby herd of pigs. When Jesus gives them permission a remarkable thing happens. The two thousand-strong herd stampede to their death. But 'Legion' is wholly restored.

Naturally, news of such a happening is quick to spread. As far as the herdsmen were concerned, this miracle was too expensive. Crowds return to see for themselves what had happened. Their response is not one of happiness because the man is healed, but fear. Who is this stranger who has come to their shores? What has become of their pigs? They decided that Jesus was just too dangerous to have around. He interfered with their property and their profits. They demand that he should leave.

The healed man, on the other hand, wants to stay with Jesus. But Jesus turns the request down, telling him rather to go home and tell his friends and neighbours what God had done. He was to be the first missionary to the Gentiles and what a story he had to tell. In the purpose of God, the whole treacherous trip across Galilee had been for this one man.

Questions

1. When those looking after the pigs ran off to tell everyone what had happened (verse 14) do you think the first thing they said was 'Legion has been healed' or 'The pigs have drowned'? What does this tell us about their priorities? Can you think of situations where you might react in the same way?

2. There is a change of strategy here for Jesus. He has usually asked those he has healed to keep quiet about it (e.g. 1:44; 3:12); why does he change his policy here?

3. When 'Legion' asks to go with Jesus he tells him to go home to his family and tell them what the Lord has done. Why do we often find it hardest to share what Jesus has done in our lives with those closest to us?

Demon possession

Confrontation with the forces of evil was at the heart of Jesus' ministry. Mark begins his account of Jesus' work with the healing of a man possessed by an evil spirit in Capernaum (1:21–28). This conflict continues throughout the gospel, culminating in the final battle on the cross. John tells us that the reason Jesus came was 'to destroy the devil's work' (1 John 3:8).

The word for 'being possessed' occurs just thirteen times in the New Testament. It was a very real but thankfully very rare experience for evil spirits to so take over a person's personality. 'Legion' has lost all sense of his own identity. His confusion comes through in his words 'My name is Legion ... for *we* are many' (verse 9).

Everyone's life has been marred and spoiled by the Devil in some way, but for this man the image of God had all but been destroyed. However, the spirits immediately recognise who Jesus is and know that their days are numbered! There is no real struggle as they realise they are powerless to resist Jesus' authority. The one who 'no-one was strong enough to subdue' (verse 4) is swiftly overcome by Jesus.

The decisive victory will take place later when, as Paul expresses it, Jesus will disarm the powers and authorities, making a public spectacle of them, 'triumphing over them by the cross' (Colossians 2:15). That victory is anticipated in this incident.

Demons are real. Jesus took them very seriously. They can affect people who allow areas of their lives to come under their influence, but the most important thing for us to know about them is that they are no match for Jesus.

What about the pigs?

Many readers of the gospel are dismayed or disturbed by the sudden destruction of these innocent animals. Why did Jesus allow this? There are several things to bear in mind.

● Firstly, we see demonstrated here, the real purpose and power of the Devil. What he did to the pigs, he wants to do to all of God's creation. His whole desire is to kill and destroy (John 10:10). Here we see evil for the destructive force it is.

- Secondly, here is convincing evidence to this shattered man (and to everyone else) that he really has been set free. It is a case of drastic measures for a desperate case. The people of the area who had previously been terrified of him, would know he was now free and they were safe.

- Thirdly, we should see a symbolic element in this incident. The destruction of the pigs is an indication of Jesus' power to destroy all that is evil or unclean. Pigs were considered 'unclean' animals by the Jews. It was a costly deliverance, but Jesus felt it was a price worth paying. These animals were being fattened up to be killed and eaten. (Two thousand pigs would not keep a country like Britain in bacon and pork for a day! It has been pointed out that the sacrifice of Gerasene is repeated every day not to restore a broken man but to provide a tasty meal!)

  God, who sees a sparrow fall to the ground, considers the life of a man of far greater worth than many sparrows.

  This incident is not an indication of Jesus' lack of concern for animals but the greatness of his concern for people, for every person, even this man.

- Finally, from a theological point of view, we need to remember that the ultimate defeat of the Devil still lay in the future. Matthew, in his account, records Legion's words as 'Have you come here to torture us before the appointed time?' (Matthew 8:29) Revelation, the last book of the Bible, tells us about this 'appointed time' when evil in all its forms will be destroyed. This exorcism illustrated the reality of Christ's victory but also the continuing power of Satan until that day of ultimate triumph comes.

Mark 5:21–43

A miracle within a miracle

In this passage two very different people emerge, both of whom are desperate for Jesus' help. He meets their need through the faith they express in him.

Returning to the shores of Capernaum, Galilee welcomes Jesus back. A huge crowd surrounds him and amongst them is an anxious father and a desperate woman. The father is Jairus, a figure of great importance in the community. He is described by Mark as 'one of the synagogue rulers'. It was his duty to take care of all the practical arrangements within the synagogue and its services – appointing the readers, choosing the preachers, caring for the building. He was an important, well-known and well respected person.

By contrast the woman is unknown and unnamed She is simply described as 'a woman'. Her condition would have made her an unwanted outcast. Under the regulations of Leviticus chapter 25, she would not have been allowed to attend synagogue services or mix with others. Anyone who touched her would have been rendered unclean also. She should not have been amongst the crowd that day. There were complicated rules as to how she should wash her clothes, where she could go and what she could do.

Jairus was concerned for his twelve-year-old daughter who is close to death. A Jewish girl was said to reach womanhood at twelve and Luke tells us that this was Jairus' only daughter (Luke 8:42). Coincidentally (?) the woman's condition had also lasted twelve years. Forgetting all prejudice or dignity Jairus falls at Jesus' feet and begs for his help. Self-importance is of little value when your only daughter is dying.

Position and wealth are no protection from sickness, but pride can prevent its cure (see the healing of Naaman in 2 Kings 5:1–14). Jesus responds immediately. They hurry off towards Jairus' home only to be delayed by the unknown woman. Jesus is as ready to respond to her need as to that of the important official. In verse 34 he even describes her as 'daughter': the only time in the gospels that Jesus ever uses this expression and probably the first time this anonymous woman had been addressed in such a tender way for many years.

It seems that Jesus is a last resort for her. She has tried everything. (It is interesting that Luke, a doctor, leaves out the reference to doctors in his account!) The Jewish Talmud listed any number of crazy and costly 'cures' for her condition. From tonics and medicines to carrying the ashes of an ostrich egg in a linen bag in summer and a cotton bag in winter, to carrying a barley corn found in the dung of a she-ass! What many doctors could not do over twelve years, Jesus does in a moment! Her healing is instant and complete.

Meanwhile Jairus stands anxiously by. 'Hurry up Jesus, she has waited twelve years, another hour won't make any difference!' As Jesus ends her twelve years of misery, it looks as if Jairus' twelve years of happiness are coming to an end. And sure enough the news comes, 'It's too late'. But Jesus is totally unperturbed. 'Don't be afraid' he tells Jairus, 'just go on believing'. Jairus' faith is being tested.

Arriving at the house they find the elaborate and noisy rituals of mourning under way already. Jesus' words seem deliberately ambiguous, 'The child is not dead but asleep' (verse 39). The word is used in the New Testament both for normal sleep and figuratively of death (e.g. 1 Thessalonians 5:10: see Acts 7:60). It makes no difference for death is no more than sleep to Jesus.

In contrast to the finality and despair of the mourners Jesus offers hope.

Quickly getting rid of the superficial mourners he goes into the child's room. Mark records Jesus' words in their original Aramaic (For other examples, 2:17; 7:11; 7:34; 14:36). 'My daughter, it's time to get up'. Everyone is amazed as she is raised to her feet. 'Don't just stand there', says Jesus, 'get her something to eat'. Jesus restores life to normal.

Questions

1. What similarities and contrasts can you see between these two interwoven miracles? Do you think there is a special significance in them happening in this way?
2. How do you think Jairus must have felt when Jesus stopped to help the woman? Compare the experience of Martha and Mary in John 11:3–6, 21.
3. Both Jairus and the woman are given as examples of faith. Compare their levels of belief; who do you think showed the most faith? Should we expect to see miracles like this today?

A healing 'touch'

We may wonder why Jesus asked the woman to make herself known to everyone. Why did he cause her such embarrassment? Could she not have slipped quietly away again healed? The answer lies in the nature of healing faith.

The faith she expresses in verse 28, 'if I just touch his clothes', is almost a superstitious one. It is faith in an object rather than a person. Faith in a 'touch' rather than in the one who is touched. Jesus brings her out into the open in order to deepen her understanding of what faith is. It is also important for the disciples to understand what has taken place.

Their response to Jesus' question, 'Who touched me?' indicates that they were unaware of what had happened. Not every physical contact with Jesus would result in healing. It was not her touch that brought healing but her faith. If she had slipped quietly away this would not have been understood.

Faith is the capacity to receive what God wants to give. It is the channel for God's blessing. Jairus had great faith. The woman's faith was smaller and slightly suspect. Jairus had faith on behalf of another. The woman had faith for herself. In both cases however, it is faith that forms the bridge between human need and God's resources.

Mark 6:1–6

The barrier of unbelief

Jesus returns to his home town of Nazareth but gets a very cool reception. This prevents him from doing all he would like to have done among them.

From Capernaum Jesus travels south with his disciples to the town where he had spent his early years and youth. Nazareth was a day's walk of some 20 miles from Capernaum.

Nazareth itself was an undistinguished place that after the time of Christ quickly sank into obscurity again. John records Nathaniel's well-known taunt 'Nazareth! Can anything good come from there?' (John 1:46). Nathaniel, to be fair, came from Cana, eight miles down the road, and village rivalry was great. But Nazareth was nothing more than a little country town in the hills of Galilee, scarcely more than a village. But it was here that Jesus had spent some thirty years of his life.

Like all male Jews, Jesus had learnt a trade. He was the village carpenter. The word Mark uses implies a craftsman rather than simply a joiner, but essentially he was a working man. The carpenter's shop was something of a centre for village life. Jesus and his family would have been well-known locally.

Just under a year ago Jesus had first returned to his home town. What happened then is recorded in Luke 4:14–30. The visit ends with him being driven out of the town and a threat to kill him. If this chronology is correct it is a powerful indication of Jesus' courage that he should return again.

On the Sabbath he is invited to speak in the synagogue to a congregation which has known him all his life. He is met with astonishment, prejudice, hostility and cold unbelief. Their reaction renders him virtually powerless. Jesus is surprised and disappointed at their response.

The root cause of their unbelief was an inadequate view of Jesus. They knew him so well, or so they thought. He was the carpenter. Their minds are full of sceptical questions: 'Where? ... What? ... Isn't?' (verses 2, 3). 'Who does he think he is?' The insinuations behind their questions are unkind and hostile. To describe a man as the son of his mother was a calculated insult, implying either that Joseph was already dead or worse, that nasty rumours were being spread about the birth of Jesus.

'He came to that which was his own, but his own did not receive him.' (John 1:11) They had grown too familiar with having the Son of God living among them. They knew him too well – but, in reality, they did not know him at all. Their failure to be open to a new appreciation of who he was limited what he was able to do.

Elsewhere, frequently we read of Jesus' powerful acts (e.g. 1:32; 6:56), even of disciples doing great things (6:12) but here Jesus' hands are tied by their unbelief. Unbelief and faith are opposites. If faith is the capacity to receive what God wants to give, unbelief is the wilful refusal to receive what God wants to give.

Faith is an open response to God's initiative but the people of Nazareth had closed minds. They erected the barrier of unbelief. Although Christ's power has no limits, the exercise of it has. Only in an atmosphere of faith and expectancy is he able to do all he wants to do. Jesus is taken aback by their response. He is 'amazed' (verse 6). That word is only used once elsewhere of Jesus, in Matthew 8:10–12, when he is 'amazed' at the faith of a Gentile centurion. A directly opposite incident.

Astonished at the faith of a Gentile, he is equally astonished at the unbelief of his own townsfolk.

Questions

1. We say 'familiarity breeds contempt'; is that a danger for us? Is it possible to become so familiar with Christian things that we lose a sense of wonder and expectancy? How can we avoid this?

2. The issue in the passage is faith versus unbelief. How would you define unbelief? Is it the same as doubt? Is God really hindered by our unbelief?

3. How could they be 'amazed' at his teaching (verse 2) and yet respond with unbelief? What does this warn us against?

JESUS' DISCIPLESHIP
TRAINING COURSE
Mark 6:7–56

The plan of Mark 3:14 begins to be put into action. Jesus puts his disciples through an intense period of 'on the job' training. Amongst the many lessons they need to learn is the vital one of trusting him as their Master.

87

Mark 6:7–13

No excess baggage

Jesus commissions the disciples and gives them guidelines for the task in hand.

Jesus' initial call to his disciples in Mark 1:17 was 'Come, follow me ... and I will make you fishers of men'. Mark 3:14 tells us that Jesus chose them with two purposes in mind. Firstly 'that they might be with him' and secondly 'that he might send them out to preach'. This is the pattern of discipleship. We are called to him, equipped by him and then sent out as his representatives.

All twelve disciples are involved, for this is not just the task of a few. Mission is the calling of all God's people. As far as the New Testament is concerned, to be a Christian and to be a missionary is one and the same thing.

They are sent out in pairs for mutual support and encouragement. This may be a reflection of the Old Testament law concerning the value of two witnesses (see Deuteronomy 17:6; 19:15). It was certainly a pattern that continued in the early church with the partnerships of Peter and John, Paul and Barnabas, Paul and Silas, etc. (Ecclesiastes 4:9–10). Such partnerships are a testimony in themselves as two lives are knit together in the service of Christ.

As Jesus' appointed representatives he gives them his authority. This is one of six Greek terms sometimes translated as 'power' in our English Bibles. The most common is *dunamis* meaning might or strength. The second most frequent is *exousia* which is the one used here. It means to have the right to something. It is used in John 1:12, 5:27, 10:18 and many other places. It speaks of power not in the sense of force but of authority. Jesus' disciples have the right to claim authority over evil spirits as his representatives. We read of them exercising this authority in verse 12.

From verse 8 Jesus gives detailed instructions as to the equipment they should take and the way in which they were to conduct their mission. They were to travel light using the minimum of provisions – no bread, no bag, no money. They were not to make elaborate preparations or be fussy about where they stayed. This was to be an exercise in faith as well as evangelism.

Many of the specific instructions are clearly for this particular commando mission. It would be foolish to apply these instructions in a literal way today. But there are principles that remain. Namely those of urgency and dependence.

Urgency means that there is no time to waste on those who are plainly not interested (verse 11). It was Jewish practice to carefully remove the dust of Gentile lands whenever they returned to Jewish soil. It was a symbol of disassociation. Paul and Barnabas use it in Acts 13:51, as they turn away from the unresponsive Jews in Pisidian Antioch.

The message is too urgent to waste time on those who are totally unreceptive. This principle has to be applied with great sensitivity and care (Matthew 7:6).

Dependence means that they are to take none of the normal resources. They are to trust God to meet their needs for food and hospitality. Hospitality was a sacred duty amongst Jews. If such hospitality was refused then it would be a clear indication that the people in that place were not ready to receive the message either.

In obedience to Jesus' command they go, even though they are only part way through their training course. Jesus is prepared to take a risk with them for two reasons. Firstly there are things they will only learn by doing and secondly the need was too urgent to wait until they have graduated from the school of discipleship (see Luke's postscript in Luke 22:35–6).

Questions

1. How do you think the disciples felt as Jesus gave them their instructions? How would they have felt when they returned afterwards? Why did he tell them to take nothing with them?

2. Jesus sent them in pairs. Usually we send preachers or missionaries off on their own and many evangelists are solo operators, is this right? How could we follow Jesus' example?

3. Which of the guidelines given in verses 8–11 are relevant to the church's mission today? How can we apply verse 11 in practice? Should we 'waste time' on unresponsive people?

Mark 6:14–29

The inside story

In this dramatic passage we are given the inside story of the death of John the Baptist. We meet the tragic figure of Herod.

The mission of the twelve disciples is causing a stir and the ripples reach the ears of Herod (see p. 93), a man haunted by a memory. In a kind of 'flash-back', Mark tells us how Herod had arrested John the Baptist and kept him in prison as a means of silencing his ministry, particularly because of John's bold condemnation of Herod's adulterous relationship with Herodias the wife of his half-brother Philip. John spoke out against such immorality. He was not afraid to condemn evil whenever he saw it. However, he was to pay the price for such fearless talk! Herodias was angry with John and looked for a way to get rid of him. Her own position was at stake. One day her opportunity came. It was Herod's birthday and with all the leading people gathered Herodias sent in her teenage daughter, Salome, to dance for them. Herodias was not above using her own daughter to trap John. Herod, probably drunk, was well pleased and made a rash promise to the girl to give her anything she might ask for. Herodias is quick to seize her chance. 'The head of John the Baptist!' Maybe it was Salome herself who added the famous touch about the platter. Herod is quickly sobered as his hilarity turns to deep sadness. He is 'greatly distressed'. This is a word Mark only uses here and in 14:34 when speaking of the sorrow of Jesus in Gethsemane.

It is an indication of the tragic complexity of this man Herod. He is at once fascinated by John but fearful of him. Although he rejects him we sense a reluctant and yet inescapable respect he has for him.

Herod is caught in Herodias' trap. He has no choice. His pride will not let him go back on his word. So, John's life ends, but his influence lives on, not least in the conscience of King Herod. As soon as word of the powerful ministry of Jesus and his disciples comes to him, he is convinced that it must be John returned to haunt him.

Herod was a man caught in two minds. Fascinated by John and his message and yet afraid of the consequences of that message for his own life. The Apostle Paul meets a similar man in authority – Felix (see Acts 24:24–26). Felix, like Herod, was fascinated but afraid. Herod's cowardice contrasts directly with John's courage.

This is the only passage in Mark's gospel that does not focus on Jesus, but the opening verses give us an insight into three popular opinions about Jesus. Some like Herod thought he was John the Baptist. This was understandable in that they preached the same message of the Kingdom of God and called people to repentance. Jesus began his ministry as John was arrested (Mark 1:14). Being cousins, they may even have looked alike. Others thought him to be Elijah, the great prophet of the Old Testament. The closing paragraphs of Malachi (4:5–6), look forward to Elijah's return to herald the close of the age. Jesus pictured John the Baptist in those terms. Others, again, thought Jesus to be another in the long line of prophets sent by God to Israel. The voice of the prophet had been silent in Israel for three centuries. Jesus spoke with authority from God.

These verdicts about Jesus recur again at Caesarea Philippi (Mark 8:27–28); they are an indication of the popularity and respect that people had for Jesus.

Questions

Reflect on the three main characters in this passage:

1. *Herod:* What kind of man was he? Do you ever find yourself in similar dilemmas – caught between conscience and life style?
2. *Herodias:* What do you make of her? Can you find anything good in her?
3. *John the Baptist:* John paid the price for his outspokenness – should he have been a little more sensitive? What are some of the issues the church should be speaking up about in society today?

Herod

It is easy to be confused by the various 'Herods' we read about in the New Testament. The marriage tangles make their relationships even more complicated to work out! The Herod here in Mark 6 is Herod Antipas who became Tetrarch of Galilee and Perea in 4 BC and ruled until AD 39. He was the son of Herod the Great who was responsible for the deaths of the young boys in Bethlehem following the birth of Jesus (Matthew 2:16).

Following his death, Herod the Great's kingdom was divided among his three sons. He gave Judea and Samaria to Archelaeus, who gained a reputation for being the worst of the lot. He had to be removed by the Roman authorities in order to prevent a full-scale revolt. The north-eastern territories were entrusted to Philip, the husband of Herodias. Galilee and Perea were governed by Antipas.

Herod Antipas had married the daughter of the Nabatean king, Aretus IV, but he sent her away in order to marry Herodias. This not only incurred the wrath of John the Baptist but also of his first wife's father. In AD 36 he waged war against Herod Antipas and heavily defeated him. Were it not for his part in the beheading of John the Baptist he would have had little place in the pages of history. The Herods were Edomites, that is, descendants of Esau, rather than pure Jews.

Herod was an insensitive and power hungry man and his disregard for Jewish sensitivity was displayed in a number of ways. For example, he chose an ancient cemetery for his capital, effectively excluding any Jew from entering it. Under pressure from Herodias he sought to be called 'King' and it was this request that led to his dismissal by the Emperor Augustus in AD 39. He ended his life in exile.

He has a brief meeting with Jesus before the crucifixion (Luke 23:7f.) and is the only person in the gospels that Jesus spoke of with what we might call contempt. He is described by Jesus in Luke 13:32 as 'that fox'.

Mark 6:30–44

An impossible situation

The disciples are confronted with a seemingly impossible situation. They have to face up to their own inadequacy to learn that Jesus is able to cope with any crises.

Jesus had sent his followers on a mission to the villages around Galilee. It had been a great success and the disciples return tired but elated to report back to him. This is the only time in Mark's gospel that the disciples are called 'apostles' (see p. 96). Sensing their weariness, Jesus invites them to have a break. He has experienced this same fatigue himself (3:20) so understands the need of his followers. A rest is called for – but it is not to be. Their hoped-for peace is quickly shattered by the demanding crowd who rush around the lake on foot and beat Jesus and his disciples to their quiet spot.

Understandably, the disciples are not pleased! But Jesus is moved with concern for the leaderless crowd. The word used to describe how Jesus felt is only used of Jesus himself in the gospels (Mark 8:2; Matthew 9:36; 14:14; 15:32). It indicated a feeling strong enough to prompt not only deep emotion but positive action. It is what the Good Samaritan experienced and expressed in Jesus' parable (Luke 10:33), a costly, self-giving compassion.

The disciples had to learn that even the most deserved rest must sometimes be sacrificed in the face of pressing need. Mark's description of the crowd as being 'like sheep without a shepherd' reminds us of the Old Testament image of God as a shepherd who leads and cares for his people (Isaiah 40:11). Jesus is God's chosen shepherd (John 10:11).

As the day draws on, the disciples begin to panic even though they had just experienced God's provision on their mission. How could such a vast number of people find food in such a remote place? The entire population of large neighbouring towns like Capernaum or Bethsaida was only between two or three thousand and Mark tells us there were five thousand men alone! With women and children the number could well have been considerably larger. It was, therefore, in many ways a sensible suggestion that the crowd should be sent on their way, but Jesus had other plans.

The disciples bring the situation to Jesus' notice and tell him what he ought to do! They must have been totally taken aback by his surprising response. 'You feed them'. 'What with?' they wonder: it would take hundreds of pounds to feed such a crowd.

We sense their irritation and a note of cynicism in their words. Where would they buy such a supply of food even if they had the money? They pluck a figure of 200 denarii out of the air, a denarius being the standard day's wage for a labourer. So 200 denarii would be the best part of a year's earnings!

As far as the disciples are concerned it was an impossible situation. The only solution was to send everyone home.

Calmly Jesus takes control. He brings the disciples back into line by telling them to divide the people into manageable groups. He wants to teach the Twelve a lesson as well as feed the five thousand. Could it be that they had returned from the mission proud of their success? It is as if Jesus deliberately puts them into a situation where they cannot cope, in order that they might learn again their total dependence upon him. They had been telling Jesus what to do, but now he brings them back into service as waiters!

Mark gives us some interesting eyewitness details as he recalls the scene. The grass was 'green', it must have been spring. The seated groups must have looked literally like 'flower beds'. Simply the miracle takes place. The way in which it happened (see p. 97) is not described, we are only told that the crowd is completely fed from five loaves and two fishes. Jesus gives the food to his disciples and they pass it out to the crowd. Everyone has enough to eat and there is even a basketful of leftovers for each disciple. The scraps were always gathered after a meal and collected in the small wicker basket that every Jew carried. This would be tomorrow's lunch.

In contrast to what has gone before, King Herod enjoys a banquet (verse 28) whilst his people are hungry. Jesus the Shepherd/King cares for and feeds his people.

Questions

1. Mark describes the crowd as 'like sheep without a shepherd'; what do you think he meant by that? Are there people in your community that could be described in this way? How can we help them to find the Good Shepherd?

2. The disciples were aware of the need but powerless to meet it, their only answer was to send the people away. How do you react when your plans are unexpectedly spoilt? What should we do when we feel overwhelmed by the needs around us?

3. What should our response be as Christians to millions who are hungry and in need in our world today?

Apostles

This title is used over eighty times in the New Testament, but this is the only time it occurs in Mark's gospel.

At the simplest level it means 'one who is sent' and it is used in this way in the New Testament, meaning simply a 'messenger' (e.g. 2 Corinthians 8:23; Philippians 2:25). It is also used of Jesus himself as the One who is sent by God (Hebrews 3:1). It is used in a special way of the twelve disciples.

Luke tells us that Jesus chose the Twelve and designated them 'apostles' (Luke 6:14). They were unique in several ways. Firstly, they had been personally called and authorised by Christ himself. The Apostle Paul speaks of a similar calling (Galatians 1:1). Secondly, they enjoyed a firsthand experience of Christ. When the early Christians want to replace Judas, who had betrayed Jesus, Peter says they must choose one 'who had been with us the whole time the Lord Jesus went in and out among us' (Acts 11:21). Again, although Paul was not one of the original Twelve and probably never saw the risen Christ in the flesh, he speaks of his experience on the Damascus road in the same way: 'He appeared to me also' (1 Corinthians 15:8).

These two qualifications set the apostles apart as unique. They have an authority that stems directly from Christ himself. They are the foundation stones of the church (Ephesians 2:20). When, in the fourth century, the church came to settle which books should be included in the New Testament and which left out, the test was whether a book stemmed from one of these unique apostles. Such books were considered to have apostolic authority.

Significantly, Mark tells us very little of how the apostles got on during their first missionary trip. More important to him is that they were sent by Jesus and return to him. This was the source of their effectiveness and their later authority.

Did it happen?

Several factors underline the importance of this incident. It is, first of all, the only miracle, besides the resurrection, that is recorded in all four gospels. Secondly, it is the most public of all Jesus' miracles.

Thirdly, Mark refers to it again in 6:52 and Jesus himself speaks of it in 8:19. It is a key miracle. But did it actually happen? One theory is that a young person in the crowd got out his lunch and began to share it with those around him. Others took their lead from his example and began to share what they had. It has been described as a 'miracle of sharing'. But this does not do justice to the account or its later significance in the gospel. Another theory is that Jesus gave all those present a token meal, anticipating the church's later practice of Holy Communion. That is, he broke the bread and fish into tiny portions so that there was a morsel for everyone. But Mark says that 'they all ate and were satisfied'. It was late in the day and the people would have been hungry.

No, this is God in action! God, who made creation out of nothing and fed his people with manna in the wilderness, now feeds his flock like a shepherd. John, in his gospel, introduces his account of this miracle with a discussion between Jesus and the disciple Philip. 'Where shall we buy bread for these people to eat?' Jesus asks him.

Then John adds this telling comment: 'He asked this only to test him, for he already had in mind what he was going to do' (John 6:6). Jesus had the situation under control. He feeds the vast crowd, and uses the disciples to do it.

Mark 6:45–56

The 'ghost' on the water

One remarkable miracle is followed by another as Jesus demonstrates his power over the forces of nature and the storms of life. But the disciples have still not learned to trust him.

This is the second time that Jesus shows his authority over the sea. The first occasion (4:35–41) focuses on the power of Jesus' word as he speaks to the surging waves. 'Quiet! Be still!' Here his whole person is involved as he walks on the water.

It has been suggested that Jesus was simply walking by the seashore and that in the uncertain light of the early dawn the disciples mistook him to be actually on the water itself. But this hardly does justice to the account here or its parallels in Matthew (14:22–33) and John (6:16–21), or to the fear they felt when they saw him. The disciples would have been relieved to see both Jesus and the shore.

The sea held particular terror for Jews, as for most ancient peoples. It was considered to be, like the wilderness, the dwelling place of demons. Isaiah speaks of it as a symbol of the restlessness of sin (Isaiah 57:20–21). The psalmist writes in a similar way (Psalm 93:3, 4). God had parted the sea to set his people free and from that point on the sea became a symbol of rebellion against God. The beast of Revelation rises out of the sea (Revelation 13:1f) and when John is given a vision of the new heaven and new earth, we are told 'there was no longer any sea' (Revelation 21:1). That final victory is anticipated here.

The disciples must have been close to the point of exhaustion as they battled against the waves. They had returned from the tiring mission hoping for a rest, only to have their peace shattered by the ever-present crowd.

Jesus, understanding their need, sends them quickly off to the other side of Galilee. It was Jesus' idea, reminding us again that the storms we encounter in life are not necessarily an indication that we are outside the will of God. John, in his account, indicates another reason for Jesus' rapid dismissal of his friends. It seems that some were so impressed by what Jesus had done that they planned to make him king (John 6:15). Jesus wanted to get away from such hero worship and did not want his disciples to be a part of such a scheme. Having sent his disciples away, Jesus himself withdrew to pray just as he did after his popular ministry in Capernaum (1:35). Whenever people tried to draw Jesus away from his Father's will Jesus took time out to pray.

Although seeking God, Jesus is not unaware of the disciples' situation and seeing their difficulties he makes his way to them. The Jewish night ran from 6 p.m. to 6 a.m. and was divided into four watches. So it would have been around 3 a.m., the darkest hour, that he came to them. At first it seemed that he was going to pass by and then they mistake him for a ghost. There was a local rumour that the last thing a boatman saw before drowning in Galilee was a ghost on the water. Quickly he reassures them with words that are reminiscent of God's revelation of himself in the Old Testament (Exodus 3:14; Isaiah 41:4; 43:10; 52:6). Their fear is replaced with amazement as Jesus gets in the boat with them and the storm dies down. They had already seen him calm a storm, now they see him trample it underfoot. The boat finds its way safely to shore.

The disciples have still not understood that they can trust Jesus in any and every situation, whether it's a hungry crowd or a raging sea.

Then Mark gives us a brief cameo of the scene in Gennesaret. No sooner do they set foot on dry land than the crowds are there again. It indicates the continuing popularity of Jesus but we are given the impression that most of them have only come for what they can get. They have little understanding of who Jesus is and what his message is all about. Jesus patiently bears with their limited understanding and responds to their needs. Significantly, there is no reference to any teaching or preaching.

Questions

1. Imagine yourself as one of the disciples. How would you respond to being caught in the storm and then to seeing Jesus apparently walking past you on the water? What lessons do you think Jesus was trying to teach his disciples here?

2. What kind of storms have you faced in your life as a Christian? How did Jesus 'come' to you?

3. Are there times when Jesus seems indifferent to the 'storms' of conflict and unrest in the world? How should we pray about them? What should we try to do about them?

More than meets the eye

Christians have always been comforted and encouraged by this incident in the gospel but it does raise some puzzling questions for us. For example, 'Why did it take so long for the disciples to cross a lake that is just a few miles wide at this point?' 'Why did he seem as if he was going to pass by?' All these questions encourage us to dig deeper and to ask what the event is trying to teach us.

The answer is surely that Jesus is wanting to teach his disciples, and us, to trust him even when he is not physically there alongside. Although at a distance on the mountainside, at prayer, Jesus is not unaware of their need. The delay in his coming to them suggests that he is trying to teach them important lessons. It was, after all, Jesus who had sent them on this trip. Several suggestions have been made as to how we should understand Jesus' apparent intention to pass them by. Firstly, that this was simply the mistaken impression that Peter had as he recalled the incident. Or, secondly, that Mark means that Jesus was going to draw alongside them. J.B. Phillips expresses it that Jesus was 'intending to come alongside'. Again, one writer even translates it 'He would gladly have passed them by', that is, he had had just about enough of them!

Perhaps the best way to understand it is to see it alongside another New Testament incident recorded in Luke 24:13–34. As the two on the road to Emmaus approach their home, Jesus, who had joined them on their journey, 'acted as if he were going further'. Without invitation the risen Jesus would not have stayed. It is, therefore, as if Jesus is saying to his disciples, 'I am here ready to respond to your call'. He offers to respond to the invitation of faith.

It is interesting to compare this incident with similar Old Testament passages – for example when God 'passes by' Moses at Sinai (Exodus 33:19, 22) and Elijah at Horeb (1 Kings 19:11). Jesus puts his divine authority at the disposal of his disciples, he is available, but he waits to be invited.

Again and again in the gospels the disciples get into a tangle when Jesus is not with them. They need to learn to trust him when he is not there for they will still be in his care, but he waits to respond to our call.

BREAKING
THE MOULD
Mark 7:1 – 8:26

There is a wonderfully unpredictable element to Jesus' ministry. It must have kept the disciples on their toes – they never knew what he was going to do next! Gradually their eyes were being opened to the truth about him.

Mark 7:1–23

God-given laws: man-made rules

A delegation of religious leaders from Jerusalem arrive to check Jesus out. The battle lines are drawn between outward religious traditions and an inward living faith.

Jesus' ministry is front-page news. Not only in the local press but also in the national dailies – news has reached Jerusalem. A delegation of experts make the one-hundred-mile journey to find out just what is going on in Galilee. The presenting issue is that of ritual cleanliness.

Mark explains it to his Gentile readers in verses 3 and 4. This was not a matter of hygiene but of religious ritual. A strict Pharisee would not only undergo this 'cleansing' before each meal but also between each course.

The Jewish Mishnah (see p. 106) contained no less than thirty chapters on the cleansing of vessels! There were also regulations covering every detail of personal hand washing. The minimum amount of water required was a quarter of a log, that is enough to fill one and a half egg shells. The water was poured over both hands with the fingers parting upwards, the water being allowed to run down to the wrists. Then the water must drop off for it is now 'unclean' having touched 'unclean' hands. The process was then repeated in the opposite direction.

Jesus rejected such elaborate external rituals. For him it was far more important that a person was clean on the inside. These ideas were not part of God's commands but the traditions of men. Jesus goes on to give another example of how they have not so much supplemented God's laws as replaced them with their own rules and regulations.

'Corban' was a technical term meaning 'devoted to God'. Jesus speaks of an irresponsible son who is fully aware that it is his duty to look after his parents in later life, but instead he declares that the money he would have used to care for them is 'Corban' – dedicated to God. In practice the money was rarely actually given. The practice was open to abuse and many sought to avoid their responsibility in this way. A 'Corban' oath was considered binding even when offered rashly. They were using this human tradition to avoid a God-given responsibility. Scrupulously observing what men commanded they subtly avoided what God required. And this was only one example of many claimed Jesus.

From the specific example Jesus returns to the general principle. What makes a person unacceptable before God is not external things like what he or she eats but internal attitudes that come out in sin. Jesus gives thirteen examples in verses 21 and 22.

The Pharisees are fighting a phoney war, dealing only with externals. Jesus wants to deal with things at a much deeper level, the level of the heart. The capacity for fellowship with God is not spoilt by outward things like unclean hands but by personal sin. It is still easy today to reduce our faith to external matters of church practice and religious rules instead of recognising it as a heart and life transforming matter of a relationship with God. The religious leaders thought that if a person kept all their many rules they would be accepted by God. It was a superficial and totally inadequate response.

Questions

1. Think about some of your views on particular issues in the church today, e.g. women in leadership, spiritual gifts in worship, Sunday observance. Are they based on biblical truth or inherited tradition?
2. Jesus was concerned about the way we care for our parents. How does this work itself out in practice?
3. Why do you think that human beings need the security of (perhaps unwritten) rules? Does freedom in Christ mean that we can do without them?

The tradition of the elders

There are of course, food laws in the Old Testament, partly for hygienic reasons and partly because certain animals were sacred in other religions. But over the years the Pharisees had overlaid the biblical teaching with a vast amount of spoken teaching or oral tradition. The aim of this teaching was to protect and apply the law of God.

During the late second century AD, these oral teachings were written down in what was called the Mishnah, a book of six divisions – agriculture, festivals, marriage, civil life, crime and ceremonies. To this was added a commentary called the Gemara. The Mishnah and the Gemara together formed the Talmud.

This vast collection of teaching contained 248 commandments ('thou shalts!') and 365 prohibitions ('thou shalt nots!').

It was handed down from generation to generation and the Pharisees came to believe that it had been given to Moses at Sinai along with the written law of the Old Testament. They were placed alongside one another and considered equally important and equally authoritative.

In practice, the Talmud with its many details tended to smother the Scriptures and outweigh them in value. As one rabbi put it, 'The Scriptures are water, the Mishnah wine; the Gemara spiced wine'. They believed Scripture and tradition to be equally ancient and equally valid.

Jesus charges them with not so much supplementing God's word with their teaching but replacing (verse 9) and even nullifying (verse 13) it. He makes a clear distinction between what Moses said (verse 10) and what they were saying (verse 11). In Matthew's gospel 'Moses said' reads 'God said' (Matthew 15:4). God's truth was being buried beneath a mountain of human tradition that was meant to protect it but was, in fact, distorting and all but destroying it.

Tradition and Scripture

Every Christian community has its tradition and much of this is of value. It would be foolish not to listen to what God has been saying to his people through the centuries. There are some Christians who seem to give the impression that God did not do or say anything between the closing of the canon of Scripture and the 1960s! But appreciating tradition for what it is, we will not put it on the same level as the Bible. We will need constantly to differentiate between that which is scriptural and therefore always authoritative and tradition that may or may not be relevant or helpful at any given time.

For example, it is scriptural that we meet for worship each Sunday but it is traditional, certainly in the UK, that we meet at 11.00 a.m. and 6.30 p.m.! Nor does Scripture prescribe what we must *do* when we meet!

Scripture is God-breathed (2 Timothy 3:16) whereas tradition is man-made. Coming from God, Scripture is primary and authoritative, whereas tradition is secondary and must remain flexible.

Valuable in its place tradition must always remain subordinate to God's word. If we are honest, some of our most cherished beliefs and priorities may be inherited from tradition rather than inherent in Scripture. We must constantly assess our traditions in the light of Scripture and the needs of the day.

Mark 7:24–30

Unusual miracle: strange setting

Jesus seems to act in very uncharacteristic ways – avoiding contact with people, speaking harshly to someone who has come to him with a need.

Jesus and his disciples are still looking for a quiet place to rest. It had been denied them at least twice and time was moving on. Two years had passed since they had begun to follow Jesus and now only one year remained before they would have to stand on their own as leaders of his church. It was important that he find a private place to teach and train them. So they cross over into Gentile country, for the only time in Jesus' ministry.

This is the only occasion that Jesus ventures beyond the border of Israel. Tyre was a Gentile city located in Phoenicia (modern Lebanon), which bordered Galilee to the north-west. It was about 30 or 40 miles from Capernaum. Tyre and Sidon were coastal towns and busy commercial centres.

Even here Jesus is confronted with desperate human need. A woman arrives at the house seeking help for her daughter who is demon-possessed. Everything Mark tells us in verse 26 stresses her non-Jewish character. She is a Gentile by both birth and culture. The Gentiles of this area were descendants of the Canaanites and had been hated by the Jews down the centuries.

It is significant that this incident should follow the previous passage because once the baby of a Gentile mother had uttered its first cry it was considered 'unclean'. Many Jews considered Gentiles as merely 'fuel for hell'. It was forbidden to help a Gentile mother in childbirth and one of the commonest terms of abuse was 'dog'.

Jesus picks this up in verse 27. What are we to make of his apparent harshness; is he reluctant to help? We do not, of course know the tone in which Jesus' words were spoken. Many commentators suggest that he spoke humorously with a smile. 'Salvation belongs first to the Jews, is it right to take food meant for the children and give it to the dogs?' He takes the edge off the word by using a word meaning 'little dogs' or 'pet dogs' rather than the normal word for the virtually wild street dogs. There is affection in his tone.

The woman rises to the occasion and with ready wit responds. 'That's true, the children have the first right to the food, but even domestic pets come in for a share of the leftovers.' This kind of speaking in riddles was common in New Testament days.

But there is more to it than humour. There are deeper reasons for Jesus' strange words. The explanation may lie in three directions:

- Firstly, concerning Jesus himself, it is a statement of his own priorities. Jesus' mission at this stage is to the 'lost sheep of Israel' (Matthew 15:24). The 'other sheep' will come later (John 10:16).

- Secondly, concerning the disciples, he is teaching another lesson, this time about discerning God's priorities and following God's strategy (Romans 1:16).

- Thirdly and most important of all, concerning the woman, he is seeking to test and strengthen her faith. Certainly, she shows great faith in coming to Jesus with her need, crossing the barrier between Gentile and Jew she clearly believed Jesus could heal her daughter. But did she know why? She probably had heard of Jesus as a healer, merely a miracle worker; that kind of faith needed to be challenged and deepened. She clearly felt no insult in Jesus' words and comes back with an open reply. There is a priority to be recognised. In a sense, Jesus wanted to give her more than she was asking for.

As well as healing, he wanted to give her a measure of understanding. God's purposes begin with Israel but do not end there.

Questions

1. This woman is often used as an example of persistent and successful prayer. What lessons can we learn from her approach and persistence? Is it ever right to argue with God?

2. Sometimes God tests our faith in order to strengthen it. Is that true in your experience?

3. Some have accused Jesus of racism in these verses – how do you respond to that criticism? Are Christians guilty of racism today?

Mark 7:31–37

'Ephphatha'

Jesus continues his travels in Gentile territory and heals a man who is unable to hear and can hardly speak. In the way he does this, he gives us an object lesson in thoughtful compassion.

 This unusual miracle is only recorded in Mark's gospel and follows a circular journey that may have taken several months. From Tyre, Jesus apparently went north to Sidon (around 25 miles) and then south-east to the Decapolis. The probable reason for this route is that Jesus wanted to avoid entering Galilee where Herod Antipas was in control and there were those there also who wished to make Jesus king. It also gave Jesus time with his disciples away from the crowds for further teaching and training.

The Decapolis was an alliance of ten free cities most of which were situated to the east of the River Jordan (see map on p. 14). They stretched from a point north-east of Galilee southwards to Philadelphia (modern Amman). Although in Gentile territory most of the cities had large Jewish communities.

A crowd brings to Jesus a man who is both deaf and suffering from a severe speech impediment. The likelihood is that he had lost his hearing rather than being born deaf, possibly through an illness or accident, for he had some speech. But he could only speak with a great effort. Mark uses an unusual word to describe the man's condition, that is probably an allusion to the promise in Isaiah 35:5–6: 'Then will the eyes of the blind be opened and the ears of the deaf unstopped. Then will the lame leap like a deer and the mute tongue shout for joy'. The fulfilment was expected when the Messiah came.

It is fascinating to watch how Jesus deals with the man because for him each person was special and deserved a unique approach. Sensitively he takes the man aside, for to be deaf and dumb was bad enough but to be unable to communicate when surrounded by a crowd is far worse. Then Jesus begins to speak to him in a language that he can hear. At first his actions may seem strange, almost disgusting, but in fact it was Jesus' beautiful way of entering this man's world. He communicates in a kind of sign language. By putting his fingers in the man's ears he illustrates that he is going to restore his hearing. By touching the man's tongue with his own spittle he identifies with the man's need for speech. Then he looks up to heaven to demonstrate where the healing is coming from. The deep sigh is a token of his identification with the man. Finally Jesus commands healing. Every touch and gesture has meaning.

Ephphatha is an Aramaic word that Mark then translates for his Gentile readers as 'Be opened'. The man begins to speak plainly. We then read Jesus' familiar instruction not to tell anyone about what had happened. He did not want his ministry hindered by those who would look upon him simply as a miracle worker and healer. This man must have found the injunction harder to obey than most! He wanted to use his new ability to speak and we can hardly blame him. The people of the region are very impressed by what they have seen but have yet to understand who it is who has done this amazing thing.

Questions

1. We live in a computer-processed society that deals in numbers, groups and stereotypes. We classify people, but Jesus saw each person as an individual. What can we learn from Jesus' approach to this particular man? Is there someone you know who is isolated in some way by a disability? How could you show God's love to them?

2. How does your church respond to the disabled? Is there more that we could do, e.g. a 'signed' service for the deaf, special facilities for physically disabled, tapes for blind people?

3. Jesus seems almost to exaggerate his actions for the benefit of this man, using visual actions to communicate effectively. What could the church learn from this for its communication of the gospel in a television age?

Mark 8:1–10

Jesus does it again

Once again Jesus shows his care for people in need. It is a further indication of both Jesus' compassion for the crowd and his patience with the disciples.

 This is the second time we read of Jesus feeding a multitude and it has been suggested that what we have in this passage is simply a retelling of the first miracle (6:30–44). There are a number of similar features – the isolated location, the use of bread and fish, the prayer of thanksgiving etc. but there are also significant differences.

Here in Mark 8 the initiative comes from Jesus himself (8:2), whereas in 6:35 it is the disciples who bring the crowd to Jesus' notice. The length of time the crowd has been with Jesus differs as does the number of loaves and fish involved. The size of the crowd itself and the number and type of baskets used to collect the leftovers is also different. In the first feeding, the disciples use twelve baskets (6:43) and the word Mark uses describes the small wicker baskets every Jew carried, the size of a lunch bag. On this second occasion they use seven large baskets of a different kind. We are in Gentile territory and these are the kind of baskets that Gentiles used made of rope or matting. They were large enough to carry a man. The Apostle Paul was let down over the wall of Damascus in a basket like this (Acts 9:25). Mark specifically describes this as 'another' occasion (verse 1) and both Matthew and Luke also record two separate feeding miracles. It would seem very strange for Mark especially, who is putting together the shortest and most urgent of the gospels, to repeat himself unnecessarily. And most significantly of all, Jesus himself speaks directly of two distinct occasions (Mark 8:19–20).

This raises the inevitable question – Why do the same thing twice? Why repeat the same miracle? Partly it was because they were in a different area. In Mark 6 the crowd would have been entirely Jews, here in Decapolis they were predominantly Gentile. But surely the basic reason is simply the compassion of Christ. A crowd was in need a second time, so Christ met the need a second time. Jesus' miracles were a demonstration of who he was but fundamentally were an expression of his love. The crowd had been with him for three days now, their own resources would have been exhausted, many of them would have been a long way from home. So Jesus feeds them and satisfies their need.

After the miracle takes place, Jesus sends them on their way and sets off by boat to an area Mark describes as Dalmanutha. Matthew describes it as 'the vicinity of Magadan' (Matthew 25:39). These are possibly two names for the same place or two towns that were close to each other on the western shore of Galilee.

Questions

1. Why do you think that having seen Jesus feed the five thousand, the disciples find it so hard to believe that Jesus can do it again? Does yesterday's miracle necessarily guarantee today's faith?

2. Sometimes we hear about 'compassion fatigue' today as we are confronted with so many needs; what can we learn from the example of Jesus?

3. There are still millions of people in our world who are hungry; what should our response as Christians be?

Mark 8:11-26

Two kinds of blindness

Jesus refuses to give the Pharisees miraculous proof of who he is and challenges his disciples to a deeper level of understanding.

Whilst Jesus gladly responded to those in need he was not in the business of producing cheap conjuring tricks. The Pharisees came looking for a 'sign' from Jesus. Mark tells us that they are out to 'test' him. They are not looking for a miracle to meet their needs but evidence of who Jesus is that can then be used against him. They want unambiguous proof of his identity. This is not the first or the last time that Jesus has to deal with this request (John 2:18; 6:30; Mark 15:32).

Jesus refuses for a number of reasons. Firstly, their motive is totally wrong – they are not looking for evidence to help them believe but to use against him. Secondly, miraculous signs are not exclusive to Jesus or an undeniable proof of divinity (Matthew 7:22, 23); a faith built on signs is always an inadequate and superficial one. But the primary reason for his refusal was that he did not perform signs to prove who he was or to coerce belief, but because he cared. His miracles were the spontaneous response of divine love to human need, not contrived actions for the laboratory. The Pharisees would only believe if he turned stones into bread or threw himself off the pinnacle of the Temple just for them (Luke 4:3, 9). Jesus is clearly saddened by their attitude and leaves rapidly. If Jesus had performed 'a sign', they would surely have wanted another one! (Luke 16:31)

Sadly, Jesus' disciples were no encouragement to him either. In their abrupt departure they forget to take any food for the journey. So following the incident with the Pharisees, Jesus takes the opportunity of teaching them a further lesson. He warns them against the 'yeast' of the Pharisees and of Herod. Yeast, in the New Testament, is almost without exception a symbol of the influence of evil (see Matthew 16:6, 11; Luke 12:1; 1 Corinthians 5:6–8; Galatians 5:9). A small amount is able to affect a large quantity of dough. (There are also references that use this idea positively e.g. Matthew 13:33.) The disciples are to be careful of the destructive influence of the Pharisees, notably, their demand for proof rather than simple faith.

It seems that the disciples misunderstand Jesus' teaching altogether. Their minds are still taken up with every-day matters like food, probably trying to work out who was to blame for not bringing the bread on board. Jesus responds with a series of questions showing how slow they have been to see the meaning behind all that has taken place. They knew all the answers – 'twelve baskets', 'seven baskets' – but they had not understood the meaning. They were like the blind man, unable to see the people for the trees! They have only begun to grasp the vague outline of Jesus and his ways.

The healing of the blind man in Bethsaida is another miracle that is only recorded by Mark. Again it takes place in private to avoid embarrassment and unhelpful publicity. The gradual healing is surely intended as a kind of parable for the disciples at this point. They are still at stage one but given time they will understand. Although the healing is gradual it is nevertheless complete (cf. Philippians 1:6). The disciples will get there in the end! Jesus will see to that.

Questions

1. Why did Jesus refuse to give a sign on this occasion when he has given so many signs already? How do we respond when people suggest that God should 'prove' himself more powerfully today?

2. What do you think Jesus meant by the 'yeast' of the Pharisees?

3. What place should 'signs and wonders' have in our presentation of the gospel today?

SHADOW OF
THE CROSS
Mark 8:27 – 9:50

Jesus and his disciples reach the crossroads. After the vital moment of recognition, Jesus begins his journey to the cross. Following this means to take the same path.

Mark 8:27–30

The fork in the road

Jesus puts his disciples on the spot. Have they grasped who he really is? Peter puts it into words for the first time.

We have reached a crossroads. About two and a half years have passed since the disciples began on their journey of discovery. Today we find out how far they have got. The events of Caesarea Philippi are a watershed, a hill top: looking back there are the crowds, the preaching, popular ministry, but looking ahead the crowds slip away, the skies darken and all roads lead to Jerusalem.

Caesarea Philippi was in the far north at the source of the River Jordan in the foothills of Mount Hermon. Jesus chose a remote and beautiful spot for this special time. Beyond Galilee, it was outside Herod's patch, in the territory of Philip. It had a somewhat chequered history. Originally known as Balina it was a great centre of Baal worship, also the site of a great temple to the Greek god Pan. It was an unexpected place for the Messiah to be recognised!

Jesus is alone with his disciples. They have walked some twenty-five miles from Bethsaida, the scene of the most recent healing miracle. Now the crowds are left behind.

The conversation begins casually with an impersonal question that was easy for them to answer. 'What are people saying about me?' asks Jesus. (It was usually disciples who asked their rabbis questions but Jesus often reversed the process.)

All kinds of rumours and opinions are in the air. Some, like Herod (6:14), thought he was John the Baptist, others that he was

Elijah. There was a widely-held belief, based on Malachi 4:5, that the prophet Elijah would return to herald in the day of the Messiah. Others, like many today, just considered Jesus to be another prophet. Current opinion was by no means unanimous but all were clearly agreed that Jesus was someone special. He has his place amongst the greatest of men. But each answer remains inadequate for Jesus is not just one of a series. He stands alone, unprecedented, unparalleled, unrivalled, unique. Have the disciples grasped this? He turns the spotlight directly on them: 'What about you? Who do you think I am?'

Peter, typically, speaks for the others when he answers, 'You are the Christ' – the Promised One! It was a moment of revelation (Matthew 16:17) and a moment Jesus had been waiting for. Significantly, he makes no attempt to deny Peter's description, but accepts his confession as true. He is the Messiah. Months of patient teaching and friendship have borne fruit. The disciples have discovered the truth about Jesus.

But then, surprisingly but understandably, Jesus tells them to keep their discovery to themselves, for at least two reasons. Firstly there were many popular ideas of the Messiah being a military or political leader, that Jesus did not fit into. He was going to enter Jerusalem, not on a noble military horse, but on a humble donkey. Clearly, Peter still had misconceptions about Jesus.

Secondly, Jesus always wanted people to discover the truth for themselves. His approach was to reveal enough evidence for faith to make its response. Those with eyes to see would recognise the truth for themselves. Jesus was not in the business of making bold statements that gave people no choice.

His way was always 'Look at the evidence – what do you think?' (e.g. see Matthew 11:2–6).

He knew that the only faith that was worth having is that which is born of conviction, not coercion. Sadly, the church has not always recognised this down the centuries. Significantly, Jesus did not sit down and say, 'I've got something vitally important to tell you today', but rather he asked them a question, wanting them to discover the truth for themselves.

Questions

1. Why do you think it took so long for the disciples to make the vital discovery of who Jesus was?

2. Who do people say Jesus is today? How can we help them to a fuller understanding?

3. Many of the great world religions accept Jesus as a 'prophet'; is this an adequate understanding of who he is? If not, why not?

The Messiah

The term 'Messiah' is found seven times in Mark's gospel, but only three times in the sayings of Jesus (9:41; 12:35; 13:21). His reluctance to use the title is probably explained by the many current misconceptions of the Messiah's role. Increasingly it had come to be used of someone who would set Israel free from her oppressors by military force.

The title itself, Messiah (Hebrew) or Christ (Greek) means 'the Anointed One' and was used in the Old Testament of kings and priests. For example, Samuel 'anoints' Saul as king in 1 Samuel 10:1. It contains the idea of being set apart by God for a particular task. In time the Jews began to look forward to *the* Anointed One who would be a great king in David's line and would bring in a new Messianic age of peace and prosperity.

Mark has no hesitancy in identifying Jesus as the Christ in the first verse of his gospel (1:1), but by then he had realised what a very different kind of Messiah Jesus was. Was Mark right? As we reflect on who Jesus was today, we shall need to consider:

● The way he came – his fulfilment of so many Old Testament scriptures.

● The words he spoke – his teaching, so clear and simple and yet full of such authority.

● The way he lived – neither his closest friends nor his bitterest enemies could find anything wrong with his character.

● The works he performed – his miracles of compassion and power.

- The way he died – this convinced a world-weary centurion (Mark 15:39).

- The way he rose again – his resurrection.

It still remains the most important question of all – 'Who do you say he is?'

Mark 8:31–38

The way of the cross

Jesus says to his disciples, 'Now you understand who I am, you must realise why I have come.' Straight away Jesus begins to talk about the cross – his and ours!

Peter, who had cleared the first fence easily, now falls disastrously at the second! But we should not be too hard on him. It is hard for us to grasp the sheer incongruity of the idea that the Messiah could suffer and be killed. It just did not make sense to Peter and the others and Peter, as usual, was not afraid to say so!

It was a shock to Peter's system and surely his words to Jesus were born of well-meaning concern. Peter had not yet grasped the fact that you don't rebuke someone you have just acknowledged to be God's Messiah! How quickly someone who is the mouthpiece of God's Spirit one minute can become a tool in Satan's hand the next.

The reason Jesus spoke so sternly to Peter was that this was the temptation that Jesus faced throughout his ministry. The lure to take an easier path and to avoid the cross. It was the test of the wilderness again, this time through the lips of a friend.

This is the first of a number of occasions when Jesus speaks about the cross (9:31; 10:33–34). As Luke tells us 'Jesus resolutely set out for Jerusalem' (9:51). There is conviction in his words that the Son of Man *must* go this way. It is an inescapable necessity, in order that the Scriptures might be fulfilled (Mark 14:21), God's purpose be achieved and humanity's need met. Jesus deliberately chooses to go the way of the cross. As if this was not enough shock for one day, Jesus has another for his disciples and the crowd.

Anyone who is serious about following him must take the same path! He begins to spell out in no uncertain terms what following him really means. Jesus doesn't promise any easy way. True discipleship is costly but worth it.

Jesus is very honest about things, he does not hide the unwelcome demands in small print. Neither does he ask anything of us that he is not prepared to give himself. He has the right to ask us to take up our cross because he has carried his own. The call to follow Jesus is not a call to give up certain things but to die. In this way Jesus sifts out the true disciples from those who are merely camp followers.

In verses 35 to 38, Jesus reminds us of factors that should be borne in mind when making up our minds whether to follow him or not. He challenges our values. If we cling on to life selfishly, asserting our rights and privileges, we lose out in the end. That kind of life is not worth having. It is foolish to sacrifice eternity for a moment.

Jim Elliott, a Christian martyr in Ecuador in the 1950s, caught the spirit of Jesus' words when he wrote in his diary, 'He is no fool who gives what he cannot keep to gain what he cannot lose.' He was twenty-two at the time and just seven years later he met his violent death. In the light of eternity things that seem so important now have no value at all.

Questions

1. We would all like to follow Jesus with no cost to ourselves; Why is that not possible? What does it mean in practice to deny oneself and take up the cross? Does Jesus ask too much of us?

2. In verse 29 Peter gets it wonderfully right. In verse 32 he gets it disastrously wrong! What lessons can we learn from this?

3. Are you aware of those who are suffering for their faith today? Do people still sometimes pay the ultimate price for what they believe? Do some research.

Son of Man

The title 'Son of Man' is one of the most common descriptions of Jesus in the gospels. It is only used once elsewhere in the New Testament, when Stephen speaks of seeing 'the Son of Man standing at the right hand of God' (Acts 7:56). Used eighty-one times in the gospels, it is never used of anyone else but Jesus and is almost without exception used by Jesus himself. It seems to have been the way in which he preferred to refer to himself. Often he uses it as a simple substitute for 'I'. For example, where Mark has, 'Who do people say I am?' (Mark 8:27), Matthew has, 'Who do people say the Son of Man is?' (Matthew 16:13). At its simplest level it can refer just to a human being, a son of Adam. It is often used in this way in the Old Testament (e.g. Numbers 23:19; Psalm 8:4). It is found in this way over ninety times in Ezekiel's prophecy. It reminds us, therefore, of the humanity of Jesus. But there is clearly more to the title than this.

In Daniel 7:13–14, the Son of Man is a title given to a heavenly figure who in the end times is entrusted by God with great authority and power. By the time of Jesus it had come to be another way of referring to the Messiah. In the years between the Old and New Testament, the Book of Enoch was written. Completed about 70 BC it contains a series of pictures of the Son of Man as a powerful central figure about to execute vengeance on the earth. He is God's special agent of judgment, a figure of fear. Again, we can understand why Peter recoiled at hearing Jesus speak of the Son of Man suffering and dying. This was something completely new.

Jesus was not afraid to use categories and titles familiar to his contemporaries but he often filled them with a very new meaning. He was going to triumph through the cross.

Mark 9:1–13

The transfiguration

In this mysterious incident, Jesus' three closest disciples are given a brief glimpse of his glory. It gives us a further insight into Jesus' place in the purpose of God.

This unique incident is recorded in all three synoptic gospels (Matthew, Mark and Luke) and there is a remarkable harmony between the accounts. The probable location was always thought to be Mount Tabor but now Mount Hermon is the more favoured site. Mount Tabor is only 1,900 ft high and Mark speaks of a 'high mountain' (verse 2). Also Mount Tabor was topped with a fortified city which would hardly give the peaceful setting Jesus required. Mount Hermon, 9,400 ft high, towers over the Jordan Valley, 11,000 ft below. It is so high that it can be seen from the Dead Sea over 100 miles away. Mountains were often special places of revelation in Scripture. It seems unlikely that Jesus and the others made their way to the very top for it would have taken some hours to climb, so the probable scene is some way up the grassy slopes of Mount Hermon.

Peter, James and John regularly emerge as an inner group among the Twelve. Not so much favourites as representatives of the others. It was clearly not easy for them to put their experience into words and the gospel writers describe what happened to Jesus in slightly different ways. Luke says 'the appearance of his face changed and his clothes became as bright as a flash of lightning' (Luke 9:29); Matthew says, 'his face shone like the sun and his clothes became as white as the light' (Matthew 17:2), whereas Mark says 'his clothes became dazzling white' (9:3).

The brightest artificial light they knew was a feeble candle or the flickering wick of an oil lamp; they knew nothing of modern powerful spotlights or floodlights, so find it hard to express the sensation of overwhelming brightness. It was a moment of spiritual illumination. The veil of Jesus' humanity was briefly drawn back and they see Jesus in a way they have not done before. Although this must have been an experience of spiritual refreshment for Jesus himself, reminding him of the glory that he enjoyed before his coming to earth and a foretaste of what was to come, it was primarily for the disciples' benefit. Mark says specifically that he was 'transfigured before them' (verse 2). It was an experience given to strengthen them for the dark days that were to come. They were given a glimpse of his glory, reminiscent of the appearances of God in the Old Testament (e.g. Isaiah 6:1–8).

Suddenly two figures step out from the pages of Scripture, Moses, representing the law, and Elijah, representing the prophets. Law and prophets together make up the Old Covenant. The three, Moses, Elijah and Jesus, represent God's dealings with mankind. It was perhaps another moment of temptation for Jesus – he was so close to home! But as the cloud of God's presence ascends Jesus remains. Deliberately choosing, not the presence of Moses and Joshua, but the chattering of Peter! The disciples are given a deeper insight as to who Jesus is and how he fits into God's unfolding plan of salvation.

The voice from heaven leaves them in no doubt. The God who had spoken in the past through the law and the prophets is now speaking decisively through his Son, they are to listen to him (Hebrews 1:1–2).

Jesus was not just successor, but superior to Moses and Elijah. He is the fulfilment of both the law and the prophets.

Peter naturally wants the moment to last. It did not occur to him not to say anything! But God's moments cannot be captured like that. The glory moments may not last, but we still have Jesus. It was an experience Peter never forgot (2 Peter 1:16–18).

Questions

1. Do you think there is any significance in the timing of this experience? How does it relate to what the disciples have just discovered?
2. What is the significance of the transfiguration for our understanding of the person of Jesus?
3. Peter wanted to preserve the moment; how do we fall into the same trap? Why is this not possible?

Mark 9:14–29

Back down to earth

Following their thrilling experience on the mountain, the disciples are confronted with a situation of desperate need. They are unable to cope because they are too busy arguing instead of praying!

 Much as Peter would have liked to, Jesus and the three disciples cannot stay on the mountain. Coming down they find the other disciples caught up in an argument with the teachers of the law and completely unable to help a father who has brought his son to them. On the mountain we are given a glimpse of Jesus' glory, here we see again the shame of human failure. It reminds us of how Jesus was thrust into the wilderness immediately after his experience of God's blessing at his baptism (1:9–13).

The incident is reported from the point of view of one of those coming down the mountain and Mark paints a very vivid picture of the scene, giving us details that are not found in Matthew or Luke. The teachers of the law are probably there to find further evidence against Jesus. The failure of the disciples would have been just what they would have been looking for! They take advantage of Jesus' absence to embarrass them.

Jesus' arrival catches everyone by surprise (verse 15). Were they just amazed to see him at that precise moment or was there something lingering about him from his recent experience? Quickly he takes in the situation and deals with it compassionately and effectively. We sense Jesus' weariness, almost exasperation, at the disciples' lack of faith (verse 19). They still have such a long way to go.

Jesus' humanity shines through as he asks how long the boy has been suffering in this way. It is clearly a serious case of spiritual oppression.

The father is desperate – is Jesus able to help? Jesus picks up on the father's words, 'if you can'. Deliverance, in this case, depends not on Jesus' ability, but on the man's faith. Faith in the right person opens up all kinds of possibilities (10:27). The father responds rapidly, expressing the measure of faith he has. We warm to his honesty for our faith is always mixed with unbelief. It is enough for Jesus to be able to act and the exorcism takes place.

At first it appears as if the boy is dead. Whether Mark means us to understand that Jesus literally raised him from the dead or it simply looked like he was dead, is not clear. Whichever, Jesus soon has him back on his feet.

Later, privately, the disciples want to know why they have failed so dismally. Jesus gives them the simple answer – in these situations the only answer is prayer. Some manuscripts add 'and fasting', but this is thought to be a later addition and is not in the best copies.

We wonder why the disciples were so useless in this situation when deliverance was part of their mandate and they had been successful in the past? (6:7, 13) Possibly the disciples had begun to rely on their own ability and past experience rather than directly on God. They were lacking in faith because they were lacking in prayer. Such powerful expressions of evil can only be dealt with by a total reliance on the unlimited power of God. Prayer is the vital link between the transforming power of the mountain top and the desperate needs in the valley. For them, as for us, prayerlessness leads to powerlessness.

Questions

1. The disciples move from glory to shame, mountain top to valley. How do our times of worship and fellowship on Sunday (or whenever) prepare us for the frustrations and challenges of weekday life?

2. Compare the father's words here (verse 23) with the leper's in 1:40. Which do you struggle with more, believing that Jesus *can*, or that Jesus *will*? Do his words in verse 23 imply that nothing is impossible as long as our faith is strong enough? What other factors should we bear in mind?

3. Does your church spend too much time in discussion and too little time in prayer? How can we correct this imbalance?

Mark 9:30–42

Teaching his disciples

Jesus takes time out to give his disciples vital teaching in the areas of humility and tolerance.

Jesus and his disciples return to Galilee: it is the first stage of his journey to Jerusalem. For a second time (cf. 8:31) Jesus speaks of his impending death, emphasising this time the part that men will play in it. He will speak of it again in 10:33–34. The disciples' failure to understand, and hesitancy to ask, underlines the sense of loneliness Jesus felt as he faced the cross. It is not that Jesus was unapproachable on the subject, but the disciples probably did not want to know too many details about what was coming – the prospect of Jesus dying was too painful.

On arrival in Capernaum, Jesus quizzes them about their conversation on the journey. We can imagine their embarrassment: it reminds us of the silence of the religious leaders (3:4). The disciples knew that what they had been talking about had been wrong and totally inappropriate for those who were following someone who was about to lay down his life for them. They were perhaps wondering who was going to take charge after he had gone. 'Who is the greatest?' 'I'll show you' says Jesus. He puts a little child before them. Greatness in the Kingdom of God is about humility and service. Later legend has it that this child became a leader in the church, possibly Ignatius of Antioch. Other stories say it was Simon Peter's son. Such suggestions are unlikely, rather it was a child, any child. We can imagine the burly fishermen, Peter and the others, the intellectual Philip, the sceptical Thomas, the zealous Simon, all standing round. Which one is the greatest? An unknown child.

Children were not given much recognition in New Testament days, but whenever Jesus wanted a child as a visual example there always seemed to be one at hand! We see Jesus sitting down here as a Jewish rabbi did to give teaching to his disciples and we can imagine him taking this young child up into his arms. The test of greatness is being ready to serve other people even if they are as 'unimportant' as a little child. Jesus turns every-day values on their head.

Alongside humility goes tolerance (verses 38–41). Aware of their special relationship with Jesus, the disciples are concerned about others acting in his name. This is the only time John is singled out in Mark's gospel although he is included with James in 10:35. It is ironic to think of the disciples forbidding others to cast out demons when they had made such a mess of it so recently!

Jesus points out that their understanding of the work of God is too narrow. Instead of writing this person off as a rival, Jesus wants them to see him as a potential ally. He is working towards the same goal. We must see Jesus' words here in the light of teaching elsewhere in the New Testament (i.e. Matthew 7:21–23; Acts 19:13–16). To use Jesus' name without understanding is to invite disaster, but the Christian will always want to affirm and encourage those who are working for good. Even the smallest act of kindness is of value in the Kingdom (verse 41). The opposite is also true (verse 42).

To cause someone to stumble is to deserve the most severe punishment. The millstone Jesus has in mind is not the small one used in the home, but one that took an ass to turn it. To be thrown in the sea with one of these tied to you only led to one result! This was in fact used as a means of capital punishment in both Rome and Palestine.

Questions

1. The disciples did not understand but were afraid to ask; are we sometimes like that? What stops us asking for the help we need?

2. 'He was not one of us' (verse 38). How often this attitude has plagued the church; can you think of examples from your own experience? Should there be limits to our tolerance however?

3. What is the modern equivalent of a 'cup of water' today? Think of some examples and then put them into practice.

Mark 9:43–50

Spiritual surgery

Jesus gives us some serious teaching about sin and its consequences. It needs radical treatment but it's very much worth it in the end.

In this passage, Jesus speaks in a vivid Eastern way about how ruthless his followers need to be with anything that draws them away from God. He tells us 'If your hand causes you to sin', that is, 'if it's something you touch', then 'cut it off', that is, 'don't touch!' Again, 'If your foot causes you to sin', that is, 'if it's somewhere you go', then 'cut it off' – 'don't go there!' Again, 'If your eye causes you to sin', that is, 'If it's something you look at', then 'pluck it out' – 'don't look!' He is not, of course, speaking literally, but he is saying in the strongest possible terms, that anything that causes us to go astray in our lives needs to be dealt with ruthlessly. Just as a surgeon sometimes has to amputate a part of the body in order to save a person's life, the same is true spiritually.

Jesus was always telling people to get rid of anything that would prevent them from following him as they should, be it possessions (10:21), family (10:28) or even life itself (8:34f). No sacrifice is too great to make in order to receive the life of the Kingdom and avoid hell.

The word Jesus uses for 'hell' is Gehenna, which is a Greek translation of the Old Testament phrase 'Valley of Hinnom'. This was a steep-sided valley on the south side of Jerusalem. In Israel's darkest days it was a centre for idol worship. Children were sacrificed to the God Molech (2 Kings 23:10). Jeremiah calls it the 'valley of slaughter' (Jeremiah 7:31–32; 19:6). By the time of Jesus it had

131

become the rubbish dump of Jerusalem. A fire consuming rubbish burned continually. The corpses of crucified criminals were literally 'thrown into Gehenna'. It was a great disgrace for a Jew to remain unburied. It was here that Judas took his life after his betrayal of Jesus (Acts 1:19).

It was, therefore, a natural image for Jesus to use to convey a place of suffering and punishment. A place to be avoided at all costs.

Verse 49 is unique to Mark's gospel and speaks of a different kind of fire, the fire of purification. Every Christian can expect to go through a sifting process and this idea would have been of particular relevance to Mark's first readers who were suffering greatly at the hand of Nero (cf. 1 Peter 1:7; 4:12).

The three sayings concerning 'salt' in verses 49 and 50, are probably best understood as three separate sayings of Jesus linked by the 'salt' idea. The first speaks, as we've seen, of the testing of the disciples lives (cf. Malachi 3:2). The second, of the need for salt to remain pure. Strictly speaking, salt cannot lose its saltiness but it can be contaminated by various impurities. If that happens it is 'good for nothing' (Matthew 5:13). The third underlines the need for purity if the Christian is to have the preserving effect in society God wants us to have. It links back with the thought of taking sin seriously and dealing with anything that is impure in our lives as decisively as possible.

Questions

1. What kind of things might you need to 'cut off' from your life really to be what God wants you to be?

2. Some have taken this as a mandate for the church, the body of Christ, to excommunicate those whose lives do not match up. Do you think that is a legitimate interpretation of the verses? What are the dangers of such a view?

3. How can we get society to take sin more seriously? Why are we afraid to speak of the reality of hell?

Hell

The idea of hell is not a popular one today. According to a survey in 1986 only 23 per cent of Europeans believe in hell. Many modern theologians feel there is no place for hell or eternal punishment in the Christian gospel.

Two alternatives have been put forward – universalism or anni-hilationism. The universalist believes that because God is love, salvation is universal, that is, everybody will eventually end up in heaven. He would appeal to Scriptures such as John 12:32; Romans 5:18; 11:32; 1 Timothy 2:3; Titus 2:11; 1 John 2:2. The annihilation view is that only Christians will live for ever, unbelievers will be totally destroyed. Key texts for this view are: Philippians 2:10f; Ephesians 1:9f; 1 Corinthians 15:28.

In fact, it was Jesus who showed us more of the love of God than anyone and who knows the heart of the Father best of all, who speaks of hell more than anyone else in the Bible. Always with great compassion and tenderness, never with harshness, but always with uncompromising directness (e.g. Matthew 5:22; 8:12; 10:28). To question the reality of hell is, therefore, to question the authority of Jesus. A loving mother will give her child honest warn-ings, 'Don't go too near the fire or you might get burned', 'Don't play in the road or you might get run over.' These are not idle threats but realistic warnings. Part of God's love for us is the honest warnings he gives.

The Bible takes sin and its consequences very seriously as this passage shows. Jesus paid for it with his life, which he saw as a nec-essary sacrifice for sin.

As modern Christians we easily lose sight of the sheer holiness of God and the utter sinfulness of men and women. What amazed the first Christians was not that God should judge sinners but that he should forgive them.

10

RELATIONSHIPS IN THE KINGDOM
Mark 10:1–52

Jesus turns many of our every-day values upside down. People and things that don't usually matter suddenly become really important. The rich and successful find themselves outside looking in.

Mark 10:1–12

For better, for worse

The Pharisees test Jesus with one of the 'hot potatoes' of the day – the issue of divorce. Jesus gives positive teaching about marriage.

The question of divorce was a burning issue in Jesus' day, as it is today. The Pharisees themselves, who put the question to Jesus, were divided over it. Some followed a rabbi, named Shammai, who took the strict line that divorce was only permissible on the grounds of adultery, whereas others followed another rabbi, called Hillel, who held a very open view allowing divorce on any number of grounds. One of Hillel's followers said a man could divorce his wife simply if he found another woman more attractive! This second, more lax view, was most popular and divorce was tragically even more common then than now.

Again, we note that the Pharisees were not so much interested in where Jesus stood on the issue but rather they were looking for more evidence for their dossier against him (verse 2). They want to test his orthodoxy. But, it is interesting that although asked about divorce, Jesus speaks first about marriage (verse 7). He begins with a very different perspective than the Pharisees. They were obsessed with the grounds for divorce; Jesus is much more concerned about the principles of marriage.

The real question for him was not the precise interpretation of a phrase in Deuteronomy 24, but 'What was God's intention for marriage in the first place?'

For the answer, Jesus takes them back to early chapters of Genesis and God's original purpose of a lifelong, exclusive relationship between a man and a woman in marriage. As far as Jesus was concerned any discussion about divorces had to be seen within this context.

God's intention is that a marriage should be a permanent commitment and anything less than that is less than God's ideal. That is all he says to the Pharisees; the teaching on divorce is given later, privately, to the disciples. Jesus cuts right across the Pharisees' preoccupation with legal loopholes and reminds them of divine principles.

There is provision for divorce in the Old Testament law. Deuteronomy 24:1 speaks of a certificate of divorce, but Jesus explains that this was a concession to human weakness and not part of God's ideal. It was not intended to encourage divorce but to allow it in certain circumstances. This was not a command from God but a concession, for human weakness and failure.

By the time of Jesus, obtaining a divorce had become a very simple affair. A bill of divorce would be written up by a rabbi, then put before the Sanhedrin. Women were left in a very insecure position. A man could divorce his wife for almost any cause whereas a woman could only ask for a divorce on the most serious of grounds. The regulations said, 'A woman may be divorced with or without her will, but a man only with his will'. Against this background, Jesus' words in verses 11 and 12 are revolutionary. Both men and women have equal rights and equal responsibilities in this matter.

To the teaching here we would need to add Matthew's account in Matthew 19:8–9 where Jesus speaks of 'marital unfaithfulness' as being a justifiable ground for divorce and Paul's teaching about the unbelieving partner in 1 Corinthians 7:10–17.

Mark probably excludes the phrase about 'marital unfaithfulness' because this would have been taken for granted. Adultery was punishable by death, under Jewish law, although this seems to have fallen into disuse by the time of Jesus. Nobody would have questioned that adultery was justifiable grounds for divorce. The Christian would want to say however, that even when divorce is justified, it is not essential. Divorce is always a tragedy and we will always want to look for forgiveness and reconciliation even when adultery has taken place.

Jesus totally rejects the loose practice of his day. Marriage must be taken very seriously by both men and women.

Questions

1. Has the church today compromised its position on divorce because of the prevailing attitude of society? How can the church maintain God's ideal and yet still show compassion for those who have been through divorce?

2. How could your church offer more practical teaching and support to those preparing for marriage or struggling with marriage difficulties?

3. Is divorce an unforgivable sin?

Divorce and remarriage

The question of divorce and remarriage remains a controversial and complex one. It is also an emotional one as it concerns people's lives and therefore requires sensitivity. Those who have not experienced the pain of a broken marriage must always be aware of this.

This is not an area where all Christians agree in detail as to how to apply the teaching of Scripture.

We would attempt the following summary:

- God's ideal is an exclusive life-long union of a man and woman in marriage.

- Divorce is a reluctant permission allowed by God because of the weakness of human nature. Divorce is nowhere encouraged or commanded in Scripture. It is allowed in certain limited circumstances.

- Divorce and remarriage are allowed on two grounds:
  a) Where a partner is guilty of serious sexual immorality (Matthew 19:1–12)
  b) When an unbeliever insists on leaving a believer because of their faith (1 Corinthians 7).

- Even when divorce is permissible it is not mandatory.

Questions remain as to how we apply these biblical principles in each case. What about those divorced before their conversion? What about the remarriage of those who have been divorced on 'non-scriptural' grounds, who come to us in repentance? Such situations will need to be considered carefully in the light of the teaching of Scripture and our need to seek to maintain a distinctive Christian position.

Christian standards are under attack in this area. The church needs to hold in tension its commitment to God's word alongside compassion for those who have failed, knowing that even if we personally have not fallen short in this area, we certainly have in another! Whilst we seek to resist the trends of society we nevertheless will seek to offer help to those who seek forgiveness and a new beginning.

Mark 10:13–16

Jesus and children

People who are unimportant to society matter to Jesus. He uses children as examples of the simplicity necessary for entry into the Kingdom.

This brief account is only given in outline. There are no details of time or place, but it stands as a telling contrast to the rich and powerful young man that we meet in the next passage.

Children were considered to be relatively unimportant in Jewish society. They were very much subject to their elders and thought to be unable to take any responsibility. We cannot be sure about the age of the children involved but the fact that Jesus took them up into his arms implies that they were quite young. Mark does, however, use the same word to describe the girl of twelve in 5:39–42. It was a Jewish custom to bring children to a rabbi to be blessed.

The disciples try to protect Jesus from this unwelcome interruption. They feel that the Master has more important concerns than to be bothered with children. Their intervention was probably well-meaning, but Jesus is cross with them. It is only in Mark's gospel that we read of Jesus being angry. The word implies both irritation and impatience. The disciples have still not understood how different things are in the Kingdom of God. They are still thinking in every-day terms about values and importance.

Not only does Jesus welcome the children but he tells his disciples that they must become like them. When the reformer, Martin Luther, read those words he objected: 'Dear God, this is too much. Have we got to become such idiots?'

Some have suggested that it was their innocence that Jesus had in mind. But this is hardly the case, as every parent knows – you don't have to teach a child to be naughty, it comes naturally! Jesus himself hints at the awkwardness of children in Matthew 11:16–17. Is it the attractive qualities of children that Jesus is thinking of? For example: their imagination, sense of excitement and eagerness to learn. These they may have but they also have some decidedly unattractive ones to go with them! Children can be selfish, short-tempered or cruel.

The most likely characteristic that Jesus has in mind is the receptiveness of a child. A child does not have the sophistication or self-sufficiency of an adult. A child is both willing to learn and ready to trust. In this sense we must be like them, for the Kingdom of God is a gift to be received, it cannot be earned or deserved. Unlike the rich young ruler children can make no false claims to God's Kingdom.

The children are blessed (verse 16) but the rich young man walks away sad (verse 22).

Questions

1. What was it about children that made them so special to Jesus and a good example for us?
2. What place do children have in your local church? Are they welcomed or merely tolerated? How can we improve things?
3. What is the prevailing view of children in society today? How does it compare with the attitude of Jesus? What action can we take to help children in need?

Mark 10:17–31

The man who had everything

We meet a person who had everything that most people want out of life, but not the one thing that really matters. Jesus makes it clear that there is a price to pay if we genuinely want to follow him.

 There is something very likeable about the man in this story. His meeting with Jesus is recorded in all three synoptic gospels. Matthew tells us he was young (Matthew 19:22), Luke tells us he was a ruler (Luke 18:18), and all three writers tell us he was wealthy! What more could a man want? This man has youth, status and riches, but he lacked eternal life.

We notice the eagerness of his approach to Jesus (verse 17); forgetting his dignity he runs and falls to his knees in the dust in front of Jesus. He has seen in Jesus the one thing that is so clearly missing from his own life. The greeting he offers is an unusual one, 'Good teacher'. It was not one that was ever used of rabbis in Jesus' day. Was it flattery, or an attempt to 'butter up' Jesus? That would seem out of character for this particular man. It seems more likely that it was a sincere comment, but that he did not understand the full implications of what he was saying. Jesus stops him in his tracks. 'Do you realise what you are saying?' 'Do you really understand what goodness is?' 'Do you really understand who I am?'

The young man's greatest mistake was to think that he could be good enough to earn acceptance with God. He stands in direct contrast to the children of the previous verses. 'Eternal life' or the Kingdom of God, is a gift to be received with child-like trust, not a reward for personal goodness.

We have no reason to doubt the integrity of his claim in verse 20, but eternal life is not something that can be achieved by human effort; it must be received by faith. God's standard of goodness is perfection, a standard that even the very best cannot reach. The rich young ruler had to learn that it is simply not possible to work your passage to heaven.

Jesus then goes on to point out where the blockage was in this man's life (verse 21). His great wealth stood between him and the surrender of his life to Christ. The issue was 'What comes first?'. For, in fact, he was breaking the first and greatest commandment, 'You shall love the Lord your God with all you've got!' His possessions were an idol to him, so in order to truly follow Christ they would have to go. He has to go *back* to being a child, before he inherited his wealth.

The same challenge remains for all who would follow Jesus – are we prepared to put him first?

To truly follow Christ is to put everything at his disposal. Sadly, rather than give up his wealth this young man gave up Jesus, and walked away. His love for his possessions was greater than his desire for eternal life. And, in contrast to so many in the gospels, this man goes from the presence of Jesus disappointed and miserable; and in spite of his love for him Jesus lets him go. He will not compromise the standards of the Kingdom, even for such a promising candidate. For this man, the price was too great; he wanted eternal life on his terms rather than God's. Clutching his possessions, he wanders sadly off, still lacking the one thing that really counts.

The disciples find this all too much. From their Jewish background, they would understand riches to be a sign of God's favour. 'Who then can be saved?' they ask.

Jesus points out that salvation for rich and poor alike is always something that God alone can do (verse 27). Jesus does not hide the cost involved in following him (verse 29), but he does encourage his disciples to assess their values in the light of eternity. Although he reassures them, he nevertheless continues to warn them what allegiance to him might entail. Persecution is part and parcel of following the Master who is on his way to the cross.

Questions

1. Many people today will describe Jesus as a 'good teacher'. Why is this an inadequate description?

2. Is it possible to be both rich and a faithful follower of Christ? Does Jesus ask for the same kind of renunciation of wealth from us? Is wealth a sign of God's blessing?

3. Jesus clearly loved this man, but nevertheless let him walk away; what does this have to say to us about our approach to evangelism?

Mark 10:32–45

Understanding the way of the cross

For a third time, Jesus speaks about the suffering that lies ahead of him. Unfortunately the disciples have still not grasped the purpose of his mission or the values of his kingdom.

Of the three recorded prophecies of his suffering (8:31; 9:31) this third one is the most detailed. For the first time Jerusalem is named as his destination, and Jesus gives more information about what will happen to him there. We sense the tension in the air as Jesus walks solemnly ahead of his disciples. Although this was a regular custom of the rabbis there is clearly more here. A sense of destiny surrounds Jesus, and this causes amazement and anxiety among his followers. This is not because of the forthcoming events in Jerusalem, but because of the bearing of Jesus. They are aware of his loneliness and courage as he confronts the cross.

Totally inappropriately, James and John come forward with their request. Matthew puts this into the mouth of their mother (Matthew 20:20–28) whereas Luke omits it altogether. Possibly it is the mention of Jerusalem that triggers off their enquiry. Maybe they thought that Jesus would take his place on the throne of the kingdom, when entering the city, and they wanted the best seats! The place of greatest honour was the seat to the right of the king, and the seat on the left was the next most important.

Having asked to share in his glory, Jesus offers them a share in his suffering. The cup was a familiar Old Testament picture of the wrath of God, and baptism a well-known image of death. Jesus is going to Jerusalem to bear the sins of men and women, and this was the cup the Father was to give him to drink (Mark 14:36).

James and John show a total misunderstanding in seeking for places of prestige and power, for Jesus was not that kind of king, and his was not that kind of kingdom. In fact, James was going to be the first, amongst the Twelve, to lose his life for Christ (Acts 12:2), whereas John was probably the last.

The other disciples are angry with James and John. Not because of their insensitivity or selfishness, but because they want the best places for themselves! They are jealous that the two brothers might have stolen one over on them. Again Jesus has to explain to them how different things are in the Kingdom of God. Greatness is not about power and prestige, but about service and self-giving love. They were acting like the Gentiles, who, as he has just told them, will be those who are responsible for his death (verse 33).

Jesus turns the value systems of the world totally upside down. The life of discipleship is to be marked with humility and service, and the supreme example of this is Jesus himself, who is about to give his life for them. The idea of a 'ransom' would have been familiar to the disciples. They were used to a price being paid to set a slave or a prisoner free, and Jesus uses this image to illustrate the meaning of his death. The Old Testament background is found in Isaiah 53, which speaks of the suffering servant of God who bears the sins of mankind. This is the way of God's Messiah.

It is encouraging to think that John finally grasps this principle (see 1 John 3:16).

Questions

1. If you could make one request of Jesus, and know that it would be granted, what would it be?
2. We are taken aback at the insensitivity of James and John, and yet have we really grasped these servant principles? How successfully does your church avoid 'power models' of leadership?
3. Is the servant model of leadership practical in secular society, as well as in the church?

Mark 10:46–52

The value of one

Even though Jesus is on the way to Jerusalem, he has time to stop and heal a blind beggar.

The story of Bartimaeus is the last miracle recorded in the gospels before Jesus enters the last dramatic week of his life. It takes place on the outskirts of Jericho, which was in Jesus' day one of the most attractive towns in Palestine. It marks the last stage of Jesus' journey south to Jerusalem. There are now just about 17 miles to go, that is six or seven hours of travelling time, until the final conflict begins.

Being Passover time the streets would have been full as everyone made their way to the city for the festival. It was Jewish law that every male Jew who lived within a reasonable distance of Jerusalem should attend. Perhaps the crowd was swelled this particular year by the presence of Jesus, as they must have felt he was taking his life into his hands, going to the festival. The drama was rapidly reaching its climax. Jesus was on the last stage of his last journey. He was going to Jerusalem, not to celebrate the feast, but to face a cross.

It so happened that Jesus passed Bartimaeus's 'patch', and the blind man was not slow to seize his opportunity. (Matthew reports that two blind men were healed. Possibly Bartimaeus was the more prominent of the two, and therefore Mark and Luke do not recall the presence of the other.) Blindness was tragically common, and robbed a man of his ability to earn a living, and therefore his only option was to beg. Bartimaeus cried out to Jesus with words that had never been used to address Jesus publicly before: 'Jesus, Son of David, have mercy on me'. It seems that this blind man could see more than others! What he had heard about Jesus of Nazareth convinced him that he was the Messiah, and able to meet his need.

The crowd considered that Bartimaeus was nothing but a nuisance. It was customary for rabbis to teach as they walked, perhaps they were not able to hear what Jesus was saying. Besides, they thought, he wouldn't be interested in a blind beggar like Bartimaeus at a time like this! But he is. Consistently, we see Jesus' concern for individuals in this gospel, whatever their situation or standing (e.g. 1:23; 1:30; 7:29; 7:35).

Bartimaeus is not easily put off. He is determined to get through to Jesus, and at last his opportunity comes. The cloak, probably used to collect money from passers-by, is thrown aside and he rushes up to Jesus unaided, it would seem.

Then Jesus asked what seems at first a very puzzling question: 'What do you want me to do for you?' Did not Jesus realise he was blind? Of course he did, but he wanted to give this man the opportunity to express his need, and therefore to express his faith (cf. John 5:6). He could have asked for money, but he asks for the ability to see. Specifically and definitely he makes his need known to Jesus.

Simply the healing takes place. As Bartimaeus's eyes are opened he sees the face of Jesus, and immediately begins to follow him. This was not always the case when people received healing. Bartimaeus follows Jesus along the road – the road to Jerusalem.

Questions

1. Jesus did not seem to hear Bartimaeus at first (verses 47–48): do you ever feel that is true when you pray? What does Jesus want us to do? (see Luke 18:1–8)

2. In spite of his impending death, Jesus makes time for Bartimaeus. What does this tell us about his priorities? How do they compare with our own? Do people get lost in the crowd at your church? What can be done about this?

3. Jesus asks Bartimaeus 'What do you want me to do for you?'. What would your answer be to that question today?

THE KING
TAKES CHARGE
Mark 11:1 – 12:44

The time has come for Jesus to put his cards on the table. Throughout his ministry he has been hesitant to reveal openly his identity as the Messiah, for fear of misunderstanding, but now it is time to make a public statement.

Mark 11:1–11

Jerusalem welcomes Jesus

Jesus arrives in Jerusalem. The way in which he enters the city is a fulfilment of prophecy, but not of popular expectations.

Jesus and his disciples enter Jerusalem via Bethphage and Bethany. Bethphage, meaning 'house of figs', is not mentioned in the Old Testament, but is, according to the Talmud, a village near Jerusalem. It was close enough to fall within a permitted Sabbath-day journey of the city, that is, less than a mile. Bethany, meaning 'house of dates', was a village on the eastern slopes of the Mount of Olives, about two miles from the city. Apparently it was here that Jesus spent each night of this last week of his life, probably staying in the home of his friends Martha, Mary and Lazarus. The Mount of Olives itself stood directly east of Jerusalem, and its 2,700 ft summit offered panoramic views of the city.

Jerusalem was the hub of Jewish life. Its estimated 25,000 inhabitants would have been increased many times over at Passover time by perhaps as many as 125,000 visitors. This was not Jesus' first visit to the city, but it was to be his last.

Jesus enters the city dramatically and symbolically, riding the colt of a donkey. Unused animals were regarded as especially suitable for special purposes (Numbers 19:2; Deuteronomy 21:3; 1 Samuel 6:7).

It seems that Jesus had made arrangements for the use of the animal earlier: if challenged, the disciples were to respond 'The Lord needs it now'. Although Mark does not quote the verse, it is clear that Jesus' action is to be seen as a fulfilment of the Old Testament promise of Zechariah 9:9. 'See, your king comes to you, righteous and having salvation, gentle and riding on a donkey, on a colt, the foal of a donkey'. It was a deliberately messianic act for all who were prepared to see it (cf. Matthew 21:4). The king was coming to the city, not on a horse, an animal of war, but on a donkey, the symbol of peace.

The crowds welcomed Jesus with a spontaneous show of enthusiasm. How deep their understanding went we cannot be sure. However, they find branches in the nearby fields to spread in his path. Only John, in his gospel, mentions palm leaves (John 12:13). These would have had to have been brought from Jericho, as they were not readily available in Jerusalem. The cry of 'Hosannah' means literally 'save now', and is used in the Old Testament of a direct appeal to the king (2 Samuel 14:4; 2 Kings 6:26). In this context it is a prayer for God to act decisively in their situation. The crowd continued to quote from the Hallel or praise psalms that were sung at the Passover (Psalm 118:25–26). It would appear to have been a genuine, yet superficial expression of enthusiasm, for once in the city the crowd quickly appears to disperse. Jesus makes his way into the Temple area, either alone or just with his disciples. There is a brief moment of peace before Jesus returns to Bethany for the night. It is the calm before the storm.

From this point onwards Mark's story slows down. He wants to pass on to us as many details as possible of this final decisive week.

For him, as for all the New Testament writers, the death of Jesus was the most important aspect of his life and ministry (1 Corinthians 15:3). There is an inevitability about all that takes place, and yet clearly Jesus is in control. He initiates this final confrontation that he knows to be the Father's will for him.

Questions

1. Do you think that the arrangement for the use of a colt was a supernatural event, or simply something that Jesus had previously arranged?

2. We can all find encouragement from the fact that Jesus enlisted the donkey in his service! Can you think of other New Testament examples of the principle of 'strength through weakness'? (See, for example, 1 Corinthians 12:5–10.)

3. Jesus entered Jerusalem, the city of peace, on a donkey and called his disciples to be 'peace-makers' (Matthew 5:9). Can acts of violence ever be right for the Christian?

Mark 11:12–25

Judgment in action

Jesus is angry when he does not find what he is looking for – fruit on a fig tree – and when he finds what he does not like – trading in the Temple courts.

It is Monday morning, Jesus and his disciples begin to make their way into the city. Matthew tells us that it was 'early' (Matthew 21:18) so it would be strange for Jesus to be hungry. There is clearly more to this incident than meets the eye.

Jesus appears to do things in this passage that seem totally out of character. Why does he curse a fig tree for not having any fruit on it when it is 'not the season for figs'? (verses 13). Fig trees around Jerusalem normally begin to grow leaves in March or April (Passover time) but do not produce fruit until June. Is this an unreasonable act, even an abuse of his supernatural power?

What happens is best understood as an acted parable, parallel to the actual parable recorded in Luke 13:6–9. A fig tree was a common image for God's people, Israel, in the Old Testament (e.g. Hosea 9:10; Nahum 3:12). When God looked for fruit from his people he found nothing but useless leaves. This tree promised fruit (even in April fig trees can bear a crop of smaller, edible fruit called 'taqsh' which were a sign of later fruit to come) but all Jesus found was leaves. Jesus is disappointed and announces God's judgment.

The context in which this happens underlines the note of judgment. Sandwiched between the curse and the fulfilment is the account of Jesus clearing the Temple.

It takes place in the court of the Gentiles, the only part of the Temple area in which non-Jews were allowed. Jesus expects to find the Temple to be a place of prayer and worship but finds it has been turned into a noisy market place.

Every visitor to the Temple was required to pay a temple tax in the special temple currency. Unscrupulous money-changers would make an easy profit changing Roman coins into Jewish shekels. Doves were the recognised offering for poor people. Again these were for sale in the Temple area but at vastly inflated prices. 'Outside doves cost as little as three and a half pence a pair, inside they were as much as seventy-five pence a pair', writes William Barclay.

Jesus is appalled by what he finds. What was supposed to be a sacred area had been turned into a bazaar and general thoroughfare. He responds with uncharacteristic aggression. It is the only violent act ever recorded of Jesus in the gospels. What he sees is an affront to God's honour.

Jesus explains his actions by referring to Isaiah's prophecy (56:7), demonstrating that what has been going on is entirely out of place, indeed a denial of the very purpose of the Temple area. A 'house of prayer' has been turned into a 'den of thieves' (see Jeremiah 7:11).

His action provokes a twofold response. The religious authorities are afraid, such a radical leader was a threat to public order; but the ordinary people are spell-bound, not so much by what he has done but by what he has said. Whereas today we would tend to be amazed by Jesus' actions, the people of his day were more taken aback by his teaching (Matthew 7:28).

The next day they find that the fig tree is totally withered, 'from the roots'. No-one will ever eat from its fruit again. God's judgment is coming on his people.

The connection between this and the verses that follow concerning faith and forgiveness would appear to be the effectiveness of faith. Someone who looks to God cannot only destroy worthless trees but remove inconvenient mountains. The view of the Dead Sea from the Mount of Olives may have triggered Jesus' illustrations. 'Removing mountains' was a recognised metaphor among rabbis to describe something that was to all intents and purposes impossible. Prayer made with faith has no limits provided it is offered without bitterness. Jesus indicates two aspects of the fruit he was looking for – faith and forgiveness. Alternatively, prayer may be the link – having passed judgment on the Temple for not being the place of prayer God intended, Jesus gives revolutionary treatment on prayer which doesn't require a temple.

Questions

1. What is your immediate reaction to what you see Jesus doing in this passage? Does it shock or surprise you? Why do you think he acted with such passion? What place should anger have in our lives?

2. What modern day practices might compare with the commercialisation of the Temple?

3. What do you make of the blanket promise of 11:24? How does it work in practice?

The cleansing of the Temple

Matthew, Mark and Luke all place this incident during the last week of Jesus' life, whereas John sets it very near the beginning of his ministry (John 2:12–16).

It is possible that John places it earlier for theological reasons, wanting to make the confrontation between Jesus and the religious practices of the day clear from the outset.

Alternatively, it is quite possible that this happened on two occasions, once at the start and again at the end of Jesus' public ministry. There are a number of differences in detail between the two events.

Mark 11:27–33

Jesus' authority is questioned

The religious authorities want to know what right he has to do what he has done, but Jesus refuses to give a direct answer.

Jesus and his disciples are back in the Temple court area. It was common for rabbis to walk around this area, teaching as they went. What looks like a deputation from the Sanhedrin confronts Jesus. All three groups that make up the seventy-strong ruling body are represented. They want to know what authority Jesus has to do what he has done, presumably in overturning the tables of the money-changers and the benches of the merchants.

At the simplest level they may want to know whether he has any kind of 'official' permission for such actions. What right has he as a private individual to do such a thing? At a deeper level, they may have understood Jesus' actions to be 'prophetic'. The prophets of the Old Testament often communicated their messages in action as well as words. What authority did Jesus have to act in such a 'prophetic' way? And behind all this there was surely a further attempt to trap Jesus by discrediting him in the eyes of the people. If he claimed to act on his own authority he would have appeared conceited and arrogant. If he claimed to act on God's authority it would have been clear evidence of blasphemy in their eyes.

Jesus puts the ball back in his opponents' court. Like an experienced politician he refuses to give a direct answer. Rather, he poses a counter-question that puts them on the spot. 'Was the ministry of John the Baptist from heaven, that is from God, or from men?' Jesus' accusers are caught in a dilemma. They have only two possible answers.

If they acknowledge that John's ministry is from God then not only will they stand condemned for their unbelief but they will need to recognise the one for whom John claimed to be preparing the way. On the other hand if they deny any divine authority to John's ministry they will lose credibility in the eyes of the people who held John in high regard: they could even end up with a riot on their hands. They duck the challenge and reply lamely that they do not know. Fair enough, says Jesus, neither will he answer their question.

What is happening here? Is Jesus simply being clever or awkward? No, he is challenging the motive that lies behind their approach and their willingness to look honestly at the evidence that stands before them. It was a common ploy amongst rabbis to answer a question with another question and the real question Jesus is asking here is – 'Are you prepared to recognise God-given authority when you see it?' Clearly they were not. They know the answer to their question if only they are prepared to admit it.

Questions

1. Are you surprised that Jesus did not give a straight answer to the question from the religious leaders? Why do you think he refused?

2. Does this in any way run counter to Peter's instructions in 1 Peter 3:15? Are there times when we should not answer people's questions about our faith?

3. How should we evaluate those who claim to speak and act 'prophetically' today? How can we tell if their message is 'from heaven or from men'?

Mark 12:1–12

The parable of the ranch

Jesus puts in a parable the sad story of Israel's rejection of God's messengers and now of God's Son. It is told not to condemn the religious leaders but as a final plea for them to think again.

This, the last parable of Jesus recorded by Mark, is an unusual one. Unlike most of Jesus' parables it has large allegorical elements. We are clearly meant to see God as the owner, the religious leaders as the farmers, the prophets as the owner's servants and Jesus as the owner's son. Jesus reviews Israel's history in a way that the Pharisees are quick to recognise, if not to appreciate.

The parable is true to Galilean life. Absent landowners were a common feature and they were often resented. It was not unknown for rent collectors to be treated badly. The continued patience of the owner is unusual however, as is his willingness to send his own son. His murder is the last straw for the owner, finally he steps in and gives the vineyard to others.

The vineyard is a common symbol for Israel, notably in Isaiah 5:1–7, and Jesus' message is clear. Over the years they have repeatedly rejected God's messages and now they are about to kill his Son. We are given an insight into how Jesus saw himself and his mission. He stands in succession to the great prophets of old but he is distinct from them. His relationship with God is different (see Hebrews 1:1–2). Jesus knew himself to be God's Son and that he was soon to face the cross.

Jesus rounds off the parable with a quotation from the Psalms. The picture is of builders who throw aside a particular stone as

157

they build, which turns out to be vital to the whole building. The 'capstone' was either a large stone that gave the line to a wall or the keystone in an archway. Either way this stone was indispensable to the stability of the structure.

The reference also adds a new dimension to the parable. The allegory ends in verse 8 with the 'son' rejected and killed. The Scripture quotation adds the element of hope and resurrection. Whenever Jesus spoke of his death he would always add the complementary truth that he would be raised from the dead. These same verses from the Psalms are referred to on several occasions in the New Testament (Acts 4:11; 1 Peter 2:4, 7; Romans 9:32, 33; Ephesians 2:20). It was clearly an image that meant a great deal to the early Christians.

The parable/allegory is a powerful demonstration of the love and patience of God. We note the owner's attention and care for the vineyard (verse 1). He buys the land, clears the ground, prepares the soil and makes provision to keep out wild animals or thieves. God has taken every care to provide for his people. He sends messenger after messenger but they are all rejected. Deliberately, repeatedly, people reject his love. They are now about to do so again as they prepare to crucify his much loved Son.

Questions

1. What stands out most from this parable for you – the generosity and patience of God, the stubbornness of humanity or the courage of Jesus?
2. The Pharisees clearly saw the truth about themselves in this story; do you think they saw the truth about Jesus as well? If so, why were they not prepared to accept it?
3. Why does Jesus compare God to an unpopular and resented person like an absentee landlord?

Mark 12:13–17

A 'no-win' situation

In the first of a series of trick questions, Jesus is asked about the rights and wrongs of paying taxes to the Roman authorities.

 Nobody likes paying taxes! This particular tax introduced by the Romans in AD 6 was especially unpopular as it was a constant reminder that they were a subject people. While Jesus was in Galilee the question did not arise, as Galilean taxes were paid to a Jewish tetrarch, but in Jerusalem this was a burning issue.

No specific town or place is given for the incident that is also recorded by Matthew and Luke. We presume that it was the Tuesday of Passion week, and that Jesus and his disciples are in the Temple precincts again. Mark records several verbal skirmishes between Jesus and the religious authorities as examples of probably what went on throughout this last week of Jesus' life. It was not so much that they were seeking his views on vital and controversial issues, but that they were out to collect evidence against him.

Again we see the strange alliance of the Pharisees and the Herodians (cf. 3:6). The Pharisees, strict separatist Jews, were totally opposed to Roman rule, whilst the Herodians gladly co-operated with it. They would have disagreed on the issue they put to Jesus and it is a measure of the strength of the opposition against Jesus that they co-operate together in setting this trap. (The word Mark uses can be used of a hunter seeking to ensnare his prey; Luke spells it out in Luke 20:20.)

They begin with flattery, perhaps intending to catch Jesus off guard and certainly trying to close off any escape route from giving a straight answer to their question.

They call him 'teacher' but they have no intention of learning anything from him! Jesus is quick to recognise their hypocrisy. He has seen it all before (cf. 8:11; 10:2) and there is a note of exasperation in his words: 'Won't you ever give up!'

The trap is inescapable as far as Jesus' opponents are concerned. If Jesus said they need not pay these taxes, the Herodians would have reported him to the governor on a charge of treason. If Jesus said they should pay this tax the Pharisees would have denounced him as disloyal to his fellow Jews and Jesus would have lost all credibility with the ordinary people.

Many Jews, particularly the Zealots, had flatly refused to pay this tribute which was a poll-tax levied on all men between fourteen and sixty-five years and all women between twelve and sixty-five. To pay the tax was felt by some to be a tacit acceptance of the Roman right to rule in God's city, Jerusalem.

Jesus asks for a denarius, the coin with which the tax had to be paid. (It is interesting to note that whenever Jesus needed a coin he had to ask for one.) The denarius was a small silver coin that was a usual day's wage for ordinary workers and Roman soldiers alike. On one side was a portrait of the emperor Tiberius and on the other the inscription, 'Tiberius, Caesar Augustus, son of the divine Augustus'. In asking 'Whose portrait is this?' Jesus is asking 'Who does this coin belong to?' Caesar has a right to that which is his. The 'give' of verse 17 is more correctly 'give back' – 'pay what is due'.

Jesus is saying that we have our obligations towards secular authorities. The follower of Jesus should be a responsible citizen. But he does not leave it there.

He reminds his questioners of a greater responsibility – our first allegiance is to God. Everything else must be seen in the light of our obligation to him (Matthew 6:33).

Caesar has his rights but they are limited. That which bears Caesar's image (the coin) belongs to him but that which bears God's image (men and women) belong to God.

Questions

1. What should the Christian's attitude be towards paying taxes and other civic responsibilities? (See Matthew 17:24–27)
2. Jesus demonstrates that there are responsibilities to the state that

do not infringe on our obligations to God (see Romans 13:1–7; 1 Timothy 2:1–6; Titus 3:1–2; 1 Peter 2:13–17). Is it ever right for a Christian to refuse to obey secular authorities? (see Acts 5:29) How does this apply to Christians who live under oppressive and unjust regimes?

3. Jesus seems to steer clear of the politics of his day – to what extent should Christians be involved in the political process today?

Mark 12:18–27

A ridiculous scenario

Having failed to trap Jesus with a political 'hot potato' the authorities try a theological one. Again Jesus responds with great skill.

This is the only time in Mark's gospel that we meet the Sadducees. They were a small Jewish party who lived mainly in Jerusalem and were involved with the administration of the Temple. An aristocratic and wealthy group, their influence far outweighed their size. They held the majority of seats in the Sanhedrin and the high priest was normally chosen from among them (see Acts 5:17). Although influential they were generally unpopular because they were prepared to co-operate with the Roman authorities.

Theologically they were conservative, accepting only the written law (the first five books of the Old Testament) as authoritative. They did not accept the oral traditions that were recognised by the Pharisees and most ordinary Jews.

Their understanding was also limited in that they had little or no room for anything supernatural. Therefore, they denied the Pharisees' belief in final resurrection of the dead as well as the existence of such supernatural beings as angels or spirits (Acts 23:8).

They seek to discredit Jesus with a fantastic hypothetical tale about an unfortunate widow. It seemed in their eyes to ridicule the whole idea of the resurrection or a life to come. The background to their story, which is surely an invented one, is the arrangement allowed under the law, whereby a man could marry his deceased brother's widow in order to continue the family line (Deuteronomy 25:5–10). If a child was born it was considered to be the offspring of the first husband. The practice, in fact, rarely took place, but the Sadducees saw it as an excellent way of showing how ridiculous the idea of a resurrection was. We imagine their smug expression as they lay out their challenge, it was, perhaps, one that had floored many a Pharisee already.

Jesus' reaction is immediate and direct. They have got it all wrong! Why? Because they overlooked two vital things – the Scriptures and the power of God. Because of their ignorance, they are making the fundamental error of measuring the life of heaven by the life on earth. Things are very different there, explains Jesus. Aspects of human life that are so important here are not relevant there. In the age to come life will be lived under new conditions – people will be like angels. (The Sadducees did not believe in angels either!)

The New Testament does not give us details about the life to come or the relationships that will be appropriate then but we can be sure that whatever has been good and valuable here on earth will be enriched in heaven. Procreation, one of the major purposes of marriage, will no longer be necessary but Paul assures us that 'love never ends' (1 Corinthians 13:8). Heaven will hold no grounds for disappointment! (1 Corinthians 2:9)

Then Jesus refers the Sadducees to the very part of Scripture that they do accept. Far from being absent in these books, the idea of resurrection is implicit in the nature of the God revealed there. He is the great 'I am'. He is the living God who will not abandon his people in death.

The hope of the resurrection rests in the faithfulness of God. The Sadducees thought that life after death was simply a continuation of this life but what the New Testament teaches is not survival but resurrection! God's people move on to a totally new kind of life, the joy of which will put even the joys of the best of earthly marriages in the shade (Psalm 16:11). It is always a mistake to create heaven in the image of earth.

Questions

1. Those with happy marriages may feel disappointed by Jesus' words (verse 25). Have they grounds for such disappointments? The New Testament gives very few details about the life to come, why do you think this is?

2. Can you think of modern equivalents of the Sadducees? Is it possible to rule out the supernatural elements of the Christian faith and still call it the Christian faith? Why do some people find the supernatural so hard to accept?

3. Some Christians lay great emphasis on the Scriptures and neglect God's power, others emphasise the Spirit to the detriment of the word of God. What are the dangers of either emphasis without the other? 'You are badly mistaken!' When should we *confront an error* like this, and when accept differing viewpoints as inevitable?

Mark 12:28–34

So near yet so far

Jesus meets a man who is on the threshold of the Kingdom, because he has grasped that love is the most important thing as far as God is concerned.

This is the last in the series of verbal scuffles that take place during Passion week. But this time things are different. We sense that we have a man here who really wants answers to the questions rather than seeking to trip Jesus up. He is impressed by what he has heard and is interested to know Jesus' opinion on an issue that was often discussed among the rabbis of the day. Which commandment matters most?

By this time the Pharisees had worked out that there were 613 commandments in all and although they were often divided into 'greater' and 'lesser' commandments, there were still plenty to choose from! Jesus does not have to think about his answer. The heart of pleasing God is to love God with everything you have and love others in much the same way.

Mark alone begins Jesus' answer with what is known as the *Shema*, named after the first word in Hebrew of Deuteronomy 6:4, which means hear. This was, and still is, a very important verse of Scripture for the Jew. It would be said faithfully twice each day in the morning and in the evening and every synagogue service would begin with it. Devout Jews would keep it in a small leather box called a phylactery (Matthew 23:5) which was worn on the forehead. It would also be fixed to the door post of every Jewish home in a box called the Mezuzah.

It expressed a truth that was at the heart of the Jewish faith, namely that the Lord was the only true God. The command to love

God flows from his uniqueness and his special relationship with Israel.

Jesus links this with another Old Testament scripture – Leviticus 19:18. Love for God must be complemented by love for our neighbour. Whether Jesus was the first to link the two commands in this way is unclear, but for Jesus both were so linked as to be inseparable. We cannot say we love God unless we love those whom he has made and whom he loves (cf. 1 John 4:20–21). Also, of course, he redefined the meaning of neighbour which had previously been understood as 'my fellow Jew' (Luke 10:25–37). For Jesus 'neighbour' was anyone in need.

Rabbi Hillel, who died in AD 10, had summarised the law: 'What you yourself hate, do not do to your neighbour'. Jesus expresses the same truth positively and links it inseparably with our love of God. A total love for God and a sensitive love for others is the essence of a life that pleases God.

The teacher of the law is pleased with what he hears. Some hear a patronising tone in his words. Is it not rather that here was a man, perhaps not alone, who has begun to become disillusioned with the complicated traditions and religious practices of the day? 'Here's a man who speaks my language', he feels as he hears Jesus' answer. Perhaps he had always thought as much and was thrilled to hear a religious teacher put it into words. The Old Testament had always taught that love was more important than sacrifices (e.g. 1 Samuel 15:22; Hosea 6:6; Proverbs 21:31), but very few had grasped it. It took a brave man to say as much in the forecourt of the Temple!

Only Mark records Jesus' response (verse 34). Jesus never says anything quite like this to anyone else. This man was on the threshold of the Kingdom because his attitude was right, and his heart was open. Jesus' words, perhaps deliberately ambiguous, were given to make him think further and hopefully turn interest into commitment, admiration into discipleship.

Questions

1. Augustine summarised the Christian ethic as 'Love God and do what you like'. Is this adequate? What place should rules have in Christian living?

2. Surely with this deep love for God, this man had done *enough* to

get into the Kingdom, hadn't he? What did he lack? What does this say to us about other religions today?

3. Do you know people who have come so far in their search for God and yet have stopped short of full commitment? How can we help them to take the final step?

Mark 12:35–44

Jesus goes on the attack

Jesus warns us against the hypocrisy of the religious leaders and points us towards an unexpected example.

In verses 35–40 Jesus criticises the religious leaders on two accounts: firstly, the shallowness of their teaching, and then secondly, the showmanship of their religious practices. The question concerning the Messiah seems a strange one to us, but is an example of Jesus taking on the 'experts' at their own game. Everyone accepted that the Messiah would be a descendant of David, but Jesus asks 'Have you ever considered the implications of Psalm 110:1? How can the Messiah be both David's son (and therefore inferior) and also David's Lord (and therefore superior)? What is the relationship between the Messiah as the son of David, and the Messiah as the Lord? You happily call the Messiah David's son, but have you thought through what you are saying?'

Jesus is challenging them to think again. Maybe their idea about the Messiah needed to change? There is apparently no reaction from the religious leaders, but the crowd enjoy every word.

Jesus' second criticism concerns their hypocritical dress and practices. The teachers of the law wore long white linen robes with fringes that almost touched the ground. It made them stand out in a crowd. It was also the kind of clothing that it was almost impossible to work in; everyone would know that they were men of wealth and leisure. They went for the seats at the front of the synagogue, facing the congregation, where they could see and be seen.

The teachers of the law were not paid a regular salary and were, therefore, dependent upon the generosity of rich benefactors. It was a system open to abuse as needy widows wanting spiritual help could easily be exploited. Finally, they offer lengthy prayers not so much to be heard by God but to be seen by others. Jesus has no time for such things.

By way of an attractive contrast Jesus notices a poor widow making her offering. There were thirteen trumpet-shaped receptacles in the Court of Women into which offerings were put towards temple expenses and to meet the needs of the poor. Many rich people were putting in large amounts but this un-named widow gave just two small coins. It was the smallest offering permissible under the law. Jesus notices and appreciates her gift, not because of the size but because of its generosity. (She could perhaps have kept one coin back for herself?) What matters in Jesus' eyes is not how much a person gives but the motive and sacrifice that lies behind it. Mark ends a chapter of conflict and tension on a note of generosity and appreciation.

Questions

1. The scribes had turned their religion into a matter of outward show and pride. Do we ever slip into the same error? Is it right for church leaders to wear special clothes and be called by special titles?

2. What principles of giving can we draw from the example of the widow? Was she being irresponsible?

3. Should those who have very little still be expected to give? Is it right to take up collections at church services?

12

THE KING
WILL RETURN
Mark 13:1–37

Mark 13 is Jesus' farewell message to his disciples. His aim is not to satisfy their curiosity about the future (or ours!) but to encourage their faith and help them face the challenges that lie ahead. The future is in his hands.

Mark 13:1–37 (1)

A solemn prophecy

Jesus warns his disciples against relying on man-made structures or religious trimmings. Instead we are to look forward to his return.

Chapter thirteen of Mark's gospel seems strangely out of place at first. We are used to an account that is full of action and incident that is now moving rapidly to its climax, but here we have the only lengthy address recorded in the gospel. It is possible that Mark has brought together a collection of Jesus' sayings about the future.

The chapter is difficult for us for two reasons. Firstly, it is full of Old Testament ideas and images that would have been very familiar to Mark's first readers but are strange and alien to us. Secondly, there are at least two strands of teaching intertwined as Jesus holds two events in focus at the same time. First of all he anticipates the destruction of Jerusalem that was soon to take place and then he overlays this with a vision of the final days of his glorious return.

Like a photographer with a modern camera that is able to focus on two things at once, Jesus focuses on the foreground (the events of AD 70) and the background (his second coming) at the same time. He sees one as the forerunner of the other, they are theologically linked, the first foreshadowing the second. In order to understand the chapter we need to hold on to this double perspective. Some of what Jesus says refers to immediate events, some to the last days and some to both.

The whole discussion is triggered off by a disciple's comment about the Temple building. Herod's Temple, begun in 20 BC and still not complete, was a magnificent building. Some of the stones were nearly 40 ft long, 12 ft high and 18 ft wide. The covered stones were reckoned to weigh 150 tons. The building covered approximately one-sixth of the city. Decorated in gold, it represented the best of human achievement in art and architecture. It is not surprising that the disciples were impressed.

Jesus' emphatic response must have seemed a sheer impossibility, but this is precisely what happened less than forty years later. The Roman emperor Titus invaded the city, fire raged through the Temple and Titus ordered the Temple buildings to be levelled to the ground.

Verses 14–20 are best understood as referring to these traumatic days. Every phrase underlines the urgency and horror of the events. The only hope was for people to run from the city. Jerusalem, a city of refuge for centuries, would not be a place of safety. The only escape was to flee to the hills. In fact, very few people took Jesus' advice and instead crowded into the city. A terrible siege took place, and according to the Jewish historian, Josephus, over a million people were killed, mostly through starvation; nearly 100,000 were taken captive. Only those who took notice of Jesus' words survived.

The phrase 'abomination that causes desolation' (verse 14) looks back to 167 BC, when a pagan ruler Antiochus Epiphanes desecrated the Temple by putting an altar dedicated to the pagan god Zeus in the Holy Place. Jesus says 'something like that will happen again'. He is probably referring to the Roman emperor Caligula, who in the year AD 40 insisted that he was a god and planned to have a statue of himself placed in the Temple. Fortunately he died in AD 41 before he could carry out his threat.

There was also a group of Zealot Jews who were responsible for a series of sacrilegious acts between AD 67 and 68. They occupied the Temple area, committing murder within its walls and set up a mock investiture of a clown as high priest. The details are not precise. Mark speaks of 'he' rather than 'it', so the likeliest suspect is Emperor Caligula.

So, Jesus begins with a solemn prophecy – Jerusalem will be attacked, the Temple will be destroyed – and it happened just as he said it would!

Questions

1. Mark 13 seems to interrupt Mark's telling of the story. Why do you think it is included just here? What is its relevance to Mark's first readers? What is its relevance to us?

2. It is easy to take pride in our religious buildings. What are the dangers of this?

3. Jesus speaks of a time of terrible suffering. Why did God allow this to happen?

Mark 13:1–37 (2)

An honest warning

Jesus warns his followers of dangers to come. They must expect opposition, because of deception and be open to the possibility of a delay in his return.

Jesus gives his disciples a threefold warning. Firstly, he speaks of the inevitability of persecution (verse 9). It is not going to be easy.

Opposition is always going to be part and parcel of following him. And this is not only going to come from expected sources like the secular authorities (verses 9–11), but also from unexpected ones like their own family (verses 12–13). Jesus is very honest with his disciples about what to expect and it was already happening as Mark wrote his gospel. Christians were being imprisoned, beaten and killed. 'Don't be surprised when it happens' says Jesus, 'it's all part of the package' (cf. 2 Timothy 3:12; 1 Peter 4:12). There will be persecution, but there is help available through the Holy Spirit (verse 11).

Such warnings may seem negative and unreal for those who have never experienced persecution for their faith, but for those who are going through it, it would have been a great source of encouragement not to give up. 'Jesus told us it would be like this, he hasn't lost control, he'll bring us through'.

The second warning Jesus gives was about the danger of deception. People will come making false claims to be the Messiah (verses 5–6, 21–23). The disciples are to be on their guard; it is all too easy to be misled by a persuasive leader making exciting claims. There were a great many false spiritual leaders around the time of Jesus and although there have been others through the centuries we should expect a further spate of them in the run up to Christ's return.

Thirdly, Jesus warns about the possibility of delay. Just because they see these things happening they are not to think that the end is just around the corner. The probability of a delay is indicated in several places (verses 7, 8, 10). The disciples are not to panic or be diverted from their task of preaching the gospel. Mark's first readers could easily have thought, as the storm clouds of persecution gathered, that this was it, Jesus' return was imminent. 'No', says Jesus, 'this is only the beginning of the end'. They are to keep serving the Lord until he comes.

For the New Testament writers the return of Jesus is always near, in that it is the next item on God's agenda, but they refuse to speculate as to actual dates and times.

For them the work of Jesus, his birth, his ministry, his death, his resurrection, his ascension and his return are all part of the one great act of God for our salvation. These events are all pages in one book and there is only one leaf left to turn.

The 'signs' Jesus speaks of here are what we should expect throughout the Christian era, but we will not be surprised if they are experienced with greater intensity during the final time before his return.

Questions

1. The Apostle Paul warns that 'everyone who wants to live a godly life in Christ Jesus will be persecuted' (2 Timothy 3:12). Is this true in your experience? How should we react when we meet opposition because of what we believe?

2. Jesus warns of 'false Messiahs'. How can we tell the true from the false when it comes to religious claims? What evidence do we see today of false prophets and heresies?

Mark 13:1–37 (3)

An exciting promise and a final warning

The dark days will come to an end – Jesus will return! Jesus' followers are to be on their guard and live in the light of his coming.

Using a patchwork of quotations and images from the Old Testament, Jesus breaks the exciting news that he will be coming back. The difficult days of persecution and deception will end when he returns. It is compelling to hear Jesus speak this way as he is about to face the cross.

Some of the details are puzzling to us, but two things are very clear. Firstly, the fact that he will return and secondly the way to prepare for this.

The doctrine of the second coming has suffered in two ways throughout the history of the church.

Some Christians have become obsessed by it and ended up with an unbalanced view, whilst others have virtually ignored it and been left with an incomplete gospel. We are not given all the details in the New Testament, but we are left in no doubt that the day of the Lord will come (2 Peter 3:3–4, 8–10).

The way to prepare for this is not to engage in empty speculation for 'no-one knows about that day or hour' (verse 32), but to be prepared. This is the recurring note throughout this chapter: 'Watch out' (verse 5); 'Be on your guard' (verses 9, 23, 33); 'Be alert' (verse 33); 'Keep watch' (verse 35); and the final challenge of the chapter is 'Watch!' (verse 37). Jesus wants his disciples to stay awake to keep their eyes on the road, to be on their toes.

He gives two short parables or similies to illustrate this. In verse 28 he speaks of a fig tree. Unlike most trees in Palestine, the fig tree loses its leaves in winter. As the leaves begin to appear again it is a sign that summer is on its way. The Mount of Olives was famous for its fig trees and as Jesus spoke at Passover time the leaves would be beginning to sprout. The disciples are to keep their eyes open for what is happening around them.

The second parable concerns a householder leaving his property in the charge of his servants while he goes away (verses 34–36). They need to be in a constant state of readiness because they do not know when the owner will return. The time references in verse 36 refer to the four watches of the night used by the Romans.

The Christian is to be ready for Jesus' unpredictable return all the time. There are signs to watch for, but they are deliberately unspecific. He will come suddenly, unexpectedly, but unmistakably. Jesus' challenge is: 'The time is unknown, but the time is near, so be ready!'

Questions

1. What does this passage tell us about Christ's second coming? Why is this aspect of New Testament teaching neglected so often?

2. Many people have speculated about the date of Christ's return (they have one thing in common – they have all been wrong!). What are the dangers of this approach? How does 'keeping watch' differ from making predictions?

3. How can we keep watch for Jesus' return and yet live a normal life? What does it mean in practice to live in the light of his return?

The return of Jesus Christ

There are reckoned to be over 250 clear references to the second coming of Christ in the New Testament. Yet it is an aspect of Christian truth that is often neglected or misunderstood. We could summarise the New Testament teaching under three headings:

1. The nature of his coming
   The return of Christ will be ...

Unprecedented   Nothing like this has ever happened before. The New Testament writers struggle to find words to describe an event that has no parallel in human history. Indeed the return of Christ will mark the climax of history. 'Then comes the end' says Paul (1 Corinthians 15:24). The curtain will fall on the drama of world history.

Unmistakable　　In contrast to the obscurity and weakness of his first coming, Jesus will return in majesty and glory. He will come 'like lightning' (Matthew 24:27) and 'every eye will see him' (Revelation 1:7). There will be no uncertainty about the fact that he has returned. Attempts to equate the second coming with the outpouring of the Spirit at Pentecost or with the coming of Christ to a believer's heart do not begin to do justice to the language of the New Testament.

Unexpected　　Jesus will return suddenly (Matthew 24:44). As in the times of Noah, people will be carrying on the normal, legitimate activities of life when it happens (Matthew 24:38). The day Christ returns will begin just like every other day. Although we are to watch for certain signs, it is foolish to try to work out dates and times. Jesus himself was unaware of when it would be (Mark 13:32).

2. The purpose of his coming
   Jesus will come:

To complete God's great plan of salvation (Hebrews 9:28)　　The New Testament sees all that Jesus has done and will do as part of one act of God. The birth, ministry, death, resurrection, ascension and return of Jesus are all pages in the same book. As only one page is left to be turned, the return of Christ is always near.

It is the next item on God's agenda. God's Kingdom, God's rule amongst men and women, will finally be established.

To judge all mankind (2 Timothy 4:1)　　Christians will be judged according to their stewardship and service (e.g. Romans 14:12; 1 Corinthians 3:13–15; 2 Corinthians 5:10) and non-believers will face the consequences of their rejection of Christ (2 Thessalonians 1:7f).

To deliver his people　　Several passages imply that the church will experience a period of particularly intense persecution immediately before Christ returns (Daniel 7:21; Matthew 24:12, 21f). When he returns Jesus will rescue his church and his people will enjoy a new experience of his presence and blessing (Revelation 21:1–4). The King will come to reign (Revelation 11:15).

3. The challenge of his coming

The teaching of the New Testament concerning the return of Christ is not given to encourage speculation, or to excite our imagination, but to challenge the way we live here and now (1 John 3:1–3). As Christians, the prospect of Jesus' return should spur us on to live holy lives and to be actively involved in service and evangelism (2 Peter 3:10–12). In the words of Augustine, 'He who loves the coming of the Lord is not he who affirms it is far off, nor is it he who says it is near; but rather he who, whether it be far off or near, awaits it with sincere faith, steadfast hope and fervent love'.

13

BETRAYED
AND DENIED
Mark 14:1–72

After a simple and loving act of devotion, Jesus' last hours are filled with betrayal, failure and rejection. With quiet dignity Jesus accepts all this as the outworking of God's purposes. He offers no resistance to his accusers but surrenders to the will of his Father.

Mark 14:1–11

Devotion and betrayal

In a context of hatred and betrayal, Mark records an act of simple and costly devotion. Whilst it is misunderstood by others Jesus receives it warmly and indicates its significance.

The last act begins. The passage begins with treachery (verse 1) and ends with betrayal (verse 11), but at the heart of it is one of the loveliest incidents in the gospel. It takes place in Bethany, just two miles from Jerusalem in the home of a man who is otherwise unknown to us, Simon the leper. He was perhaps a well-known victim of leprosy who had been healed by Jesus. Simon was a very common name.

It is Passover time and the streets of the city would have been crowded with pilgrims but in the privacy of Simon's home Jesus finds a quiet place. Mark does not name the woman, but John in his gospel tells us that it was Mary, the sister of Martha and Lazarus, who carried out this costly act of devotion (John 12:3). The perfume is described as 'pure nard' (verse 3), an oil extracted from a root grown in India. It was kept in a sealed alabaster flask, the long neck of which would need to be broken to release the perfume. It was possibly a family heirloom, perhaps even her dowry, and certainly worth a great deal, more than a year's wages (verse 5). Normal hospitality required a footwashing and perhaps a few drops of relatively inexpensive perfume. This was an act of extravagant love. This woman was prepared to 'waste' her most precious possession on Jesus.

Her action inevitably provokes misunderstanding and criticism from 'some of those present' says Mark. Matthew identifies them as the disciples (26:8), John singles out Judas (12:4–5). It was customary to give gifts to the poor at Passover. But Jesus is quick to defend her actions (verses 6–9). In his eyes what she has done is 'beautiful'.

Jesus' response does not imply a lack of concern for the poor but a simple recognition of an act of pure devotion. It may be foolish but it was sincere. Love does not always stop and think, it gives recklessly, sometimes without counting the cost. He also recognises how appropriate her action is at this time (verse 8). The opportunity to help the poor would always be here but the chance to help this 'poor' man would soon be gone. It would not be possible to make such a generous act for much longer.

It was the normal Jewish custom to anoint a body for burial (see 16:1), except in the case of a criminal. Jesus knew he was about to die a criminal's death. Mary's act will never be forgotten. Why did she do it? Perhaps we can suggest two reasons:

- *She recognised who Jesus was.* The eastern custom was that if a vessel was used to serve a distinguished guest it should then be destroyed in order that it was never used for anybody of lesser importance. Mary knew there would never be anyone more important than this.

- *She realised what Jesus was going to do.* Did her love give her an insight that was hidden from others concerning his forthcoming death?

In stark contrast to the selfless devotion of Mary, Mark records the bitter treachery of Judas: a cold and deliberate act of betrayal.

The authorities needed the help of the informer because of Jesus' popularity with the vast crowds, who were in Jerusalem to celebrate the feasts. Mark only gives us the bare outline of Judas' act. Matthew tells us that the money involved was 'thirty silver coins' (Matthew 26:15), the current selling price for a slave.

Questions

1. Do you feel that what Mary did was 'over the top'? Is it possible to give too much to Jesus? What is the most precious thing you could give to him?

2. Is it right for the church to spend money on expensive and elaborate places of worship when there are so many in the world who are poor? Does this incident have something to say about this?
3. Why do you think Judas did what he did?

Judas Iscariot

It has puzzled many people why Jesus chose someone whom surely he knew would betray him. It is impossible for us to finally unravel the complex interplay between God's purpose and human free will that went on in Judas' mind. One clue, it has been suggested, may be found in his title 'Iscariot'.

This is generally understood as meaning 'Man of Kerioth' which made Judas the only non-Galilean among the Twelve. He was in that sense different, perhaps he always felt the odd one out. There are indications in John's gospel of his critical nature and that he was guilty of pilfering some of the money entrusted to him (John 12:1–8). In the end he betrayed Jesus for a bag of silver. Was money the motive for his action? Or was it jealousy or fear? Here was a way to save his own skin as the end drew near.

One suggestion has been that Judas grew impatient and wanted to force Jesus' hand. That is, to put Jesus into a situation where he would have to show himself to be the Messiah. He thought Jesus needed a push and he was prepared to give it. But this theory will not fit.

It presents Jesus as being uncertain of his destiny and that Judas was simply misguided rather than guilty of a terrible sin. We ought not to doubt the sincerity of Jesus' call to Judas. He surely viewed Judas as a potential disciple alongside the others. No other interpretation does justice to Jesus' character or his repeated appeals to Judas. Judas began on the same footing as the others but slowly became disappointed and disillusioned. The disappointment gave way to resentment which allowed him to become a pawn in the Devil's hand.

It remains a warning to all of us that it is possible to be close to Jesus but not at one with him. Judas shared Jesus' company but not his spirit.

Mark 14:12–26

The Last Supper

Jesus shares a final meal with his disciples. Having often spoken of his death he now demonstrates its meaning. He is God's Passover Lamb.

As the end draws near Jesus is anxious to spend a final few hours with his friends. It was to be a farewell meal, but also much more. Careful arrangements had already been made and were now put into action. Throughout this last week of Jesus' life we sense he is always totally in control.

Two disciples, Luke tells us they are Peter and John (22:8), are sent to prepare the meal. There are parallels here to the arrangements in Mark 11:1–7. They are to look for a man carrying a water jar. This would be very unusual as they were usually carried by women. You were far more likely to see a man carrying a wineskin!

Larger Jewish houses would have upper rooms that were approached via an outside staircase. These were often used as store rooms or guest rooms, or, more significantly, as a quiet place where a rabbi could teach his disciples. It has been suggested that this may have been the house of Mary, the mother of Mark. We know that Mary lived in or near Jerusalem and that she was reasonably wealthy. The early Christians often met in her home (Acts 12:12). Did Mary send her son Mark to fetch a jar of water while she made preparations for the meal? Wherever it took place, Jesus had clearly pre-arranged all that was necessary.

The Passover meal was eaten in the evening and was a long and elaborate affair. Every aspect of the meal was full of meaning. Originally it was eaten standing, but by the time of Jesus it was eaten

185

reclining. Jesus fills the familiar elements with new significance.

He takes the Passover bread, breaks it and asks them to see it not just as bread but as a symbol of his body. He then asks them to eat it. Next he takes the cup of Passover wine and asks them to see it not just as wine but as a symbol of his blood. After a prayer of thanks, they are asked to drink it as 'my blood of the covenant' (verse 24). Passover and covenant are two of the keys he gives them to unlock the mystery. In the Passover it was the 'poured out' blood of a sacrificed lamb sprinkled on the doorway that saved the family from death. It was the body of the same lamb that was eaten by the family as they celebrated their deliverance.

Jesus begins to point to truths that will be more fully explored later in the New Testament – deliverance from death through his sacrificed body and shed blood. This makes a new covenant or agreement between God and humanity. Much of this must have been unclear to the disciples that evening but would have taken on an even richer meaning as they looked back on it after his death and resurrection.

It is within the context of this intimate last meal that Jesus tells them that one of them will betray him. Jesus knew what was going to happen and makes a last appeal to Judas. His treachery remains hidden from the others. The dipping of bread into a bowl of sauce was a common practice and a token of friendship (see Psalm 41:9).

When it was over they sang a hymn, probably one of the Hallel psalms (Psalms 113–118) and made their way towards the Mount of Olives.

Questions

1. What does the Lord's Supper mean for you personally and as a church? Review the way your church obeys the command of Luke 22:19. Could you 'remember' the Lord better?
2. Has the church lost some of the simplicity of the communion service over the centuries? How could this be recaptured?

Mark 14:27–31

Pride before a fall

Jesus tell his disciples that they will all let him down. Peter and the others are quick to protest but Jesus rapidly punctures their self-confidence.

 A subdued and reflective group of disciples follow Jesus out of the city along the valley towards Gethsemane. They do not return to Bethany on this last evening before the festival. Jesus breaks the heavy silence with a solemn prediction. Basing his words on Zechariah 13:7, he tells them that they will all turn their backs on him, but when it is all over they will be reunited in Galilee.

Their failure will not take Jesus by surprise and it is one of the clearest indicators of the courage of Jesus that throughout these last days of his life he was fully aware of what was going to happen. He knew that just when he needed them most of his friends would let him down.

Peter, as so often, speaks up boldly. We sense a certain offence behind his words and a vehemence in his voice. Even if all the others drop away, he will not. Again, it is an indication of the integrity of Peter that he ensures that Mark records his proud words. He did not have any difficulty in thinking that what Jesus said could be true for the others! Sadly, Peter will speak with a similar intensity shortly in denying Jesus (14:71).

Jesus underlines his reply with 'I tell you the truth', an expression he often uses when he wants to emphasise his words (see 3:28; 8:12; 9:41; 10:15, 29; 11:23; 12:43; 13:30; 14:9, 18, 25, 30). Not only will Peter fail him, he will do so three times before the night is over.

The time is defined with pin-point accuracy, 'today', i.e. during the course of this very night. The second cock-crow was proverbial for marking the early dawn. Some have suggested that Jesus may have been referring to the bugle call that was sounded in the city to mark the changing of the guard. The third watch of the night was called 'cock-crow'. It seems more likely however, that Jesus has the morning call of the rooster in mind. The threefold denial emphasised how total Peter's failure was going to be.

Peter is a central figure to Mark's account of Jesus' death and resurrection. He is noticeably asleep (14:37) and follows at a distance (14:54). The details of his denial are included in 14:66–72. We can imagine Peter re-living these events as he tells them to Mark. Not least the words of the risen Christ (16:7).

There is a certain irony in Peter insisting that he is prepared to die with Jesus when he had earlier tried to turn Jesus away from the cross (8:32). Had he at last begun to grasp something of the ways of Jesus? We should not doubt the honest intent of Peter and the others to remain faithful to Jesus, they surely meant what they said. But only Jesus knew how tough it was going to be for them.

Questions

1. How do you think the disciples felt when Jesus told them they would fall away? Why did he warn them in advance that this would happen?
2. What was the root of Peter's final failure: pride? self-confidence? fear? over-emotional love? lack of understanding? What can we learn from his experience?
3. Did the disciples *have* to fall away in order to fulfil the Scriptures?

Mark 14:32–42

The real battlefield

We are given an intimate insight into the suffering of Jesus and his relationship with the Father. In Gethsemane the real battle was fought and won.

Jesus and his disciples make their way to Gethsemane, a garden or orchard on the lower slopes of the Mount of Olives. The name means 'olive' or 'oil press', that is, a place where the oil was squeezed from the olive. It was one of Jesus' favourite places (Luke 22:39), somewhere they had visited before. Judas clearly knew where to find them.

Jesus wanted to pray, so leaving the other eight disciples he takes Peter, James and John further into the garden. These three seem to have been an inner core of the disciples (cf. 5:37) but it is particularly appropriate that they should be present now. It was these men who had been guilty of rash self-confidence when Jesus had spoken of his suffering: James and John (10:38–40); Peter (14:29, 31). How would they respond to its harsh reality?

Jesus becomes greatly distressed, he tells his disciples that his 'heart is ready to break with grief' (NEB). This is no play acting, the anguish Jesus experienced is intensely real. He cries out to God: 'Is there any other way?' It is not that Jesus is afraid of death or the process of dying but he is painfully aware of what his death will entail. He will be giving his life as 'a ransom for many' (10:45). He will, in the words of Paul, become 'sin for us' (2 Corinthians 5:21). One who had lived every moment of his life in fellowship with God his Father was about to experience total separation from God (cf. 15:34). Jesus is asking if there is any other way that sinful men and women can be reconciled to God other than by his drinking the cup of God's wrath and judgment.

Within the intensity of this situation he speaks to God as 'Abba, Father'. This is something totally new. There is no evidence in Jewish writing of the time of God ever having been addressed in such a personal way before. To the Jews it would have seemed irreverent, even blasphemous. But here, above all places, Jesus was aware of his special relationship with God. A relationship now made possible for all his followers (Matthew 6:9).

Returning to his disciples he finds them asleep. Not only is he looking for their support, he is more concerned for their own well-being. He does not ask them to pray for him but to pray for themselves, aware of the test they are about to face. How typical of Jesus that in this moment of intense personal conflict he should be concerned for his friends! He is aware of their weakness.

Three times he goes away to pray. For Jesus victory in prayer was not achieved in a moment. But always he expresses his trust in the Father's will. Gethsemane is a place of honesty and intensity, but above all surrender. Jesus submits to the Father's will as being the only way that his task of salvation can be achieved.

The 'enough' of verse 41 is decisive. It can mean in business terms, 'the bill is paid': everything is settled, the transaction has taken place. Satan's hour has come but Jesus emerges from the garden already having won the battle.

In contrast to Jesus' sleeping disciples, his enemies are very much awake and active. Jesus turns to face them secure in the Father's will.

Questions

1. This is the third time that Mark records Jesus praying (cf. 1:35; 6:46). What common threads are there between the three situations? What lessons about prayer can we learn from this passage?

2. Jesus looks for support from his friends but fails to get it. Have you ever been let down by your friends in this way? What can we learn from Jesus' dependence on his Father?

3. Jesus commits himself to God's will. Are there times when you struggle with accepting God's will for your life? Why do we so often find ourselves resisting God's will?

Mark 14:43–52

Jesus is arrested

Led by Judas, the authorities arrive to arrest Jesus. The disciples desert him and Jesus is left alone.

Judas knew where to find Jesus and as the night grows darker he arrives with a body of men. They have a warrant for Jesus' arrest issued by the Sanhedrin, the most powerful Jewish court. Mark lists the three component parts of this governing body in verse 43. John tells us there were Roman soldiers among the group also (John 18:3) and the mention of clubs suggests local conscripts. We are given the impression of a rabble hurriedly brought together for the purpose.

Mark pointedly reminds us that Judas was one of the Twelve, but he shows little interest in Jesus' betrayer. He is not mentioned again after this point. Judas' treachery is set in stark relief by the warm greeting and familiar kiss. 'Rabbi!', the Hebrew term for teacher, was the normal way a disciple would have addressed his master and a kiss was a customary mark of respect. These tokens of devotion were turned to symbols of treachery as a pre-arranged sign for Jesus' opponents.

Without delay the arresting party move in to arrest Jesus. The only show of resistance is from one of those present who draws his sword and severs the ear of the servant of the high priest. John tells us it was Peter and that the servant's name was Malchus (John 18:10). It is the kind of impulsive act that it is easy to believe that Peter would have been capable of and reminiscent of Moses' rash violence (Exodus 2:12). Perhaps Mark thought it was too dangerous to reveal Peter's identity as he wrote, whereas when John was recording these events Peter had already died a martyr's death.

Only John and Luke mention the healing of the ear, and that it was the right ear.

Jesus offers no resistance to his arrest and does not want any well-meaning interventions on his behalf. There is, in fact, a certain irony in his words as he smiles at his assailants. 'What's all this about? Here you are with swords and clubs as if I was some violent criminal who has been successfully avoiding capture for months. You could have arrested me any time. In fact, this is all part of God's plan.' He has Scriptures such as Isaiah 53:12 and Zechariah 13:7, in mind.

Then, just as Jesus had said (verses 27–31) the disciples run for their lives. We sense Mark's sadness as he recalls 'everyone deserted him and fled' (verse 50). 'Even me!' if, as is widely suggested, the mysterious reference to a young man in verses 51 and 52 refers to Mark himself. These verses are unique to Mark and are thought by many to be John Mark's way of saying 'I was there!' The 'linen garment' was an outer cloak made of wool and the description implies that the owner came from a wealthy family. The fact that the young man, probably in his teens, fled naked suggests he may have dressed quickly to witness the scene. Jumping out of bed he had not bothered with underclothes but simply threw his outer garment on. Maybe he had come to warn Jesus of the betrayal that had taken place, but arrived too late? Maybe he had come simply to see what was going on? Perhaps, if it was Mark, he had intended to follow Jesus and is telling us with sad honesty, 'In the end even I ran away'. Jesus faced his trial and execution alone.

Questions

1. What do you make of Judas? How could he spend so long in the company of Jesus and then turn against him? Are there lessons for us here?

2. Peter tried to defend Jesus in an appropriate way by the use of violence; is it ever right for Christians to take up arms in the defence of their faith? Are there other inappropriate ways of defending Jesus' cause?

Mark 14:53–65

A kangaroo court

Jesus' case is given a preliminary hearing before the Sanhedrin, but they have already made up their minds that he must die. The outcome is a foregone conclusion.

Jesus is led back into the city to the home of the high priest, Caiaphas, although Mark does not mention his name. Caiaphas was the son-in-law of Annas, the previous high priest, and he held office for nineteen years (AD 18–37). Considering that the average length of time at this stage was two years, it is an indication of his ability and influence.

Mark tells us that Peter followed 'at a distance'. At least he was there whereas the other disciples were nowhere to be seen. Only Mark mentions the fire in the courtyard. He will tell us more of Peter shortly.

The background to the various trials recorded in the gospels is the problem the Jewish leaders faced. They had decided that Jesus must be killed but they did not have the authority under Roman law to carry out such a sentence. They needed to find a charge that would carry weight in a secular court. This initial hearing appears to be an attempt to piece together a worthwhile case.

Various witnesses are brought forward but their testimony is totally unconvincing. Jewish law required the unanimous evidence of at least two witnesses (see Deuteronomy 17:6; 19:15; Numbers 35:30). The fact that such witnesses were so readily available points to pre-planning on the prosecution's behalf. But they had not briefed their informants well enough.

Mark picks out one particular accusation (verses 57–59). The destruction of a place of worship was regarded as a capital offence.

Perhaps some had heard Jesus' words recorded in Mark 13:2, concerning the destruction of the Temple, or more likely his words in John 2:19. It was only after the resurrection that the disciples realised he was not talking about the Temple in Jerusalem but the temple of his body (John 2:21–22). Jesus may have said similar things on other occasions. His accusers seized on his words but even then could not agree about what he had said.

At last Caiaphas decides to take matters in his own hands. Under the law Jesus was required to answer the accusations made against him but he refused to do so. As far as he was concerned there was no case to answer. Defence would have been futile in such an atmosphere and might only have provided further ammunition for the opposition. Behind Jesus' silence is a quiet acceptance that this is the will of God for him. It is a silence of faith.

Caiaphas grasps the nettle. He gets up from his seat and throws a direct question at Jesus. 'Do you claim to be the Messiah?' Such a leading question was forbidden but Caiaphas is frustrated, perhaps angry. Jesus answers simply 'I am'. The reserve and secrecy is put aside, it is time for plain speaking. Jesus backs up his words with Scripture, bringing together Psalm 110:1 and Daniel 7:13. In contrast to the person they see in chains before them, one day they will see him as he really is! Those who now judge him will see him as the Judge of all people.

This is too much for Caiaphas; by tearing his clothes he demonstrates that he considers Jesus' words blasphemous. There was no further need for witnesses or questioning. Jesus had condemned himself as far as the high priest was concerned: this was blasphemy! And the penalty for blasphemy was death by stoning! (Leviticus 24:16) They had all they needed, all that was required was a rubber stamp from Pilate.

Questions

1. Why do you think Jesus remained silent when he knew the accusations were false? Should we do the same when it happens to us?

2. Why did Jesus bring the proceedings to a conclusion by providing the pretext for the death penalty when they couldn't cobble a case together themselves?

3. For reflection: 'Bearing shame and scoffing rude,
In my place condemned he stood.'

Mark 14:66–72

Peter hits rock bottom

With simple honesty Mark records Peter's denial of Jesus. In spite of Jesus' warning Peter fails disastrously.

Even as Jesus faces mockery and abuse in an upstairs room, downstairs in the courtyard one of his most faithful friends disowns him. Mark takes up the story from verse 54. As Peter warms himself by the fire one of the female servants of the high priest speaks to him. 'Your face looks familiar.' Perhaps she had seen him with Jesus earlier. We sense that Peter is not only in the wrong place but in the wrong company.

There is contempt in her voice as she describes Jesus as 'that Nazarene'. Peter denies the charge with words that are a formal, legal denial. 'I do not know what you are saying – not guilty.' Having done so, Peter decides to find a less conspicuous position in the entrance area. But the servant girl is not easily put off and begins to share her suspicion with others. Again Peter directly denies any connection with Jesus.

Time passes but soon Peter's accent gives him away again. Galileans were easily identified by their local dialect. This time the challenge is more emphatic! 'Surely you are one of them?' It provokes an equally aggressive response from Peter. 'May God punish me if I'm not telling the truth, but I swear I don't know this man.' Peter cannot bring himself to use Jesus' name. He is angry and afraid, caught up in a mixture of emotions. At that moment, as Peter denies all knowledge of Jesus for a third time, the cock crows and he recalls Jesus' words. His anger turns to tears. Luke tells us that Jesus caught Peter's eye at this point (Luke 22:61).

No doubt Peter recalled his rash promise, his proud self-confidence; it was as if all that he had learnt over the years was forgotten in a moment.

Some early manuscripts mention at the end of verse 68 that a cock crows after the first denial. It has been observed that the cock usually crows three times during the night in Jerusalem. Firstly, about half an hour after midnight, then about an hour later and then about an hour later again. Each crowing lasts about 3–5 minutes and then it is quiet again. About an hour would have passed between Peter's first and third denial. It was Peter's darkest hour.

A well-known statue of Peter has him holding a bunch of keys in one hand and a cock behind his back in the other. It is this mixture of courage and cowardice, of success and failure, which makes Peter so attractive to us. We can readily identify with him.

It is a tribute to Peter's honesty that he insists on Mark recording these events that can only have been spoken of by Peter himself. Peter was not too proud to let the world know about his failure. Peter fell despite years of being with Jesus and being told exactly what dangers he would face (verses 27, 30) and how to avoid them (verses 37, 38). He failed because he was too sure of himself (verse 25), too careless (verse 37) and perhaps too fond of his own comfort (verses 54, 67). He remains as a warning to us.

Yet failure was not the end. The risen Christ forgives and restores Peter (16:7; John 21:15–19). But for now we see a big man in tears.

Questions

1. Are you surprised by the way Peter acted? What were the main factors that led up to his failure? Are you ever tempted to be ashamed of Jesus?

2. How is Judas' betrayal different from Peter's denial? Why did Peter find his way back whereas Judas did not?

3. Mark records Peter's tears. Are we afraid to express such emotion in the church today?

14

FROM FRIDAY TO SUNDAY
Mark 15:1 – 16:8

With moving simplicity, Mark tells the story of Jesus' trial, execution and resurrection. It is an account of the darkest night and the brightest dawn told plainly and convincingly. The gospel ends on the familiar note of wonder and amazement.

Mark 15:1–15

On trial

The Jewish leaders bring Jesus to be tried by Pilate, the Roman governor.

 The working day began at daybreak and the decision made during the night hours is quickly ratified by the whole Sanhedrin. It is now Friday of Passion week. Jesus' accusers needed a more substantial charge than blasphemy to put before the Roman authorities, so they refine it to a charge of treason. Mark only gives us the story in outline (note the 'many things' of verse 3): we have to turn to the other gospels for more detail.

Pilate became governor of Judea in AD 26 and remained in office until AD 36. He was largely unpopular because he showed little or no understanding of Jewish sensitivities. The charge of claiming to be king of the Jews, a secular understanding of the Messiah, would have been delivered to Pilate and when the hearing gets under way Pilate comes straight to the point. Jesus' reply is deliberately vague, 'You have said it'. It is neither a denial nor a straightforward acceptance, for Jesus is the King of the Jews but not in the sense that Pilate is using the words (see John 18:33–37).

As various accusations are thrown at Jesus he remains silent (Isaiah 53:7). Such silence is unnerving and unusual for under Roman law a prisoner who made no defence was considered to be guilty. But very quickly Pilate concludes that Jesus, to his mind, is not so much a revolutionary leader as a religious fanatic. Convinced of his innocence he tries two ploys to get Jesus acquitted.

Firstly, he remembers an apparent custom of releasing a Jewish prisoner at Passover time.

There is no evidence for such a custom outside the New Testament but there are parallels elsewhere in Roman law. Pilate clearly hoped the people would ask for Jesus. He was wrong.

Nothing else is known of Barabbas or the insurrection that he was involved in, but there were any number of such uprisings around this time. It is possible that Barabbas had a number of supporters in the crowd that day who had come to Jerusalem especially for the Passover amnesty. They were quick to take advantage of the situation. It was not that Jesus was unpopular with the ordinary people, but that he was with the religious authorities. Barabbas was more their kind of 'Messiah' – a popular freedom fighter.

His first attempt having failed, Pilate tries a different approach. He appeals to the crowd, 'What shall I do with your king?' They promptly respond 'Crucify him!' 'Why? What has he done wrong?' Pilate pleads, but the crowd were not interested in justice, they want blood. Perhaps a lesser punishment will satisfy them?

In the end Pilate gives in to the fanatical crowd. He releases Barabbas and has Jesus flogged. For this a whip made of strips of leather embedded with pieces of bone and lead was used. The Jews set a limit of forty strokes but the Romans set no such limits and many victims died from such a punishment.

Finally, Pilate 'delivers' Jesus over to be killed. The word Mark uses here appears regularly in his gospel (1:14; 9:31; 10:33; 14:10, 11, 18, 21, 41, 42, 44; 15:1, 10, 15) and recognises that these events are not just the acts of sinful men but the working out of the purpose of God. The background is found in Isaiah 53:12, which in the Greek version reads, 'He bore the sins of many and was delivered because of their iniquities.'

Questions

1. Mark's first readers were experiencing persecution and facing trials at the hands of the Roman authorities; how would Mark's account of Jesus' trial be a source of encouragement and help to them? Does it help you when you face opposition for your faith?

2. What makes people do things in a crowd that they might never agree to do in the cold light of day? To what extent do we find ourselves carried along by the views of those around us? Find examples.

3. Pilate comes through to us as a weak figure. Why do you think he acted in the way he did? What can we learn from him about the dangers of compromise?

Mark 15:16–32

The King is crucified

Mark tells the story of Jesus' journey to the cross. Surrounded by insults and abuse, Jesus dies in quiet dignity. We watch and worship.

It was all in a day's work for the soldiers, but it was not every day they had someone who claimed to be a king to make fun of. They relieve their boredom with a few minutes entertainment at Jesus' expense. The purple robe was possibly an old military cloak, its colour suggesting royalty. The crown of thorns was a cruel caricature of the wreath worn by the emperor. They mockingly pay homage to him, the act of spitting a parody of the kiss normally offered to a king. It was a cruel pantomime, cynical, brutal, unnecessary. Christians who have faced jeering and laughter for their faith down the centuries have only experienced a part of what their Lord endured.

Normally those condemned to crucifixion carried their own crossbeam, perhaps weighing as much as 40 pounds, to the place of execution. Jesus was clearly too exhausted to do so, and a passer-by was press-ganged into doing so. Simon of Cyrene was probably a Jewish pilgrim who had come to Jerusalem for the festival. Cyrene was a city in North Africa with a large Jewish population. Only Mark records that he was the father of Alexander and Rufus; perhaps they were well-known figures to Mark's first readers. Paul writes of a Rufus in Romans 16:13, as 'chosen in the Lord' and this may be the same man. Some have wondered if the 'Simeon called Niger' of Acts 13:1 is the Simon, but this is only speculation.

It was both Roman and Jewish practice to carry out executions outside the residential part of the city (see John 19:20). Golgotha, the place of the skull, may refer to a skull-shaped rock or simply be the name given to it because of the many crucifixions that took place there. It was Jerusalem's 'killing field'.

Death by crucifixion was one of the cruelest and most humiliating ways of being killed. It was reserved for slaves and violent criminals: a Roman citizen could not be crucified. Mark, like all the gospel writers, is restrained in his account, refusing to dwell on the pain of the nails or the shame of Jesus' nakedness. A mix of wine and myrrh was a traditional way of easing pain, but Jesus refuses it. Then says Mark simply 'they crucified him'.

Normally the victim was stripped and his outstretched arms were nailed or tied to the crossbeam. The cross-piece was then fastened to an upright stake forming a T-shape. A block of wood half-way up the post supported the body. Crucifixion was essentially death by exhaustion and asphyxiation.

It was accepted practice for the soldiers to divide the victims clothes between them and it was customary for the condemned man to carry a board in front of him with the charge written on it. This was then nailed above his head on the cross. 'THE KING OF THE JEWS' would have meant one thing to the Romans (a political revolutionary) and another to the Jews (a false Messiah).

Mark tells us nothing about the others who were crucified alongside Jesus (see Luke 23:39–43 , Matthew 27:44), but it is more likely that they were political activists than petty criminals for robbery was not a capital offence. But he does tell us of the continuing abuse that Jesus had to endure from passers-by and religious teachers alike. It seems that the crucifixion had attracted quite a crowd. For them it was laughable that a powerless man on a cross could be called the King of the Jews.

Questions
1. Why do you think Mark made so much of the mockery and abuse Jesus endured? (There may be a clue in Psalm 22:6–8) Does it help you when you face ridicule for what you believe?
2. Why did Jesus refuse the wine and myrrh? Would it have been wrong for him to lessen some of the pain?
3. Mark's account of the crucifixion is very restrained, why do you think this is? Is it right for preachers to major on the physical sufferings of Jesus in order to move people to respond to the gospel?

Mark 15:33–41

The torn curtain

Mark records the death of Jesus. The cross reveals the true horror of humanity's sinfulness and the full measure of God's love.

 At noon, when the sun is normally at its brightest, a sudden darkness comes across the land. Luke tells us directly 'the sun stopped shining' (Luke 23:45). Whether this was through natural means, a wind-blown dust cloud, or direct supernatural intervention, Mark intends us to see it as a sign from God. The darkness lasts for the three hours of Jesus' crucifixion. It recalls the plague of darkness recorded in Exodus 10:21–29, a sign of God's judgment. 'Outer darkness' is one of the expressions Jesus used to describe hell – total separation from God.

The symbol is confirmed by the only words of Jesus from the cross that Mark records. Taken from Psalm 22, they indicate the separation from the Father that Jesus experienced as he took the consequences of human sin upon himself (2 Corinthians 5:21). He is drinking the cup of God's wrath that he accepted in the Garden of Gethsemane (cf. Isaiah 59:2). Having gone through the rejection of the crowds and the failure of his friends, on the cross Jesus was forsaken by God himself as he took our sin upon himself. There is an authenticity in his words that reflect the harsh reality of sin and the real cost of our forgiveness.

Those standing by misunderstand his cry and think he is calling out to Elijah for help. Common belief held that Elijah would come to help an innocent victim at a time of special need. In response to this, one of the soldiers offers Jesus a drink of wine vinegar, a common drink amongst soldiers and workers (cf. Numbers 6:3; Ruth

2:14). It seems to have been a genuine offer of support rather than a cynical gesture.

Victims of crucifixion could take many hours or even days to die, with long periods of exhaustion and unconsciousness, but Jesus' death was different. He remained conscious and in control throughout the whole ordeal and died with a cry of triumph on his lips (see John 19:30).

As Jesus dies, Mark records that the curtain of the Temple was torn in two. There were, in fact, two great curtains hanging in the Temple. An outer curtain separated the sanctuary from the public forecourt and a second inner veil partitioned off the Holy of Holies itself. We cannot be sure which curtain Mark has in mind. The tearing of the outer curtain would have been a more public event but the rending of the inner veil would have been more meaningful. Whichever is in view, the message of the curtain was the same – 'No Entry! Keep Out'. The way into the presence of God was blocked and barred. Just one person, the high priest, was allowed to enter the Holy of Holies once a year on the Day of Atonement. The tearing of the curtain is Mark's vivid way of telling us that the way to God is now open (see Hebrews 9:8–10, 12; 10:19–20). The fact that it was torn from top to bottom indicates not only the completeness of Jesus' sacrifice on the cross but that this was something that God did. Jesus may have died at the hands of cruel men but the New Testament is clear that this is the outworking of the eternal purpose of God. The way to God is now open.

And the first to find that way is an unexpected figure, a Gentile centurion who had no doubt seen many crucifixions in his time. But this was different. He is deeply moved by what he has seen. His words are in some ways the climax of the gospel (cf. 1:1). This man has seen what so many religious people have missed. It is unlikely, however, that he understood the full meaning of what he was saying.

Whereas Jesus' disciples had failed miserably, the women amongst his followers remained loyal. They were eye witnesses to his death, his burial (15:47) and his resurrection (16:1).

Questions

1. How do you understand Jesus' cry of destitution (verse 34)? Luke and John leave it out of their account; why do you think they did so?

2. How does the cross demonstrate the true horror of sin and the full extent of God's love?

3. What was the significance for Mark's first readers of a Roman centurion being the one to recognise Jesus as the Son of God?

Mark 15:42–47

A borrowed tomb

Having died a lonely death, Jesus is given an honourable burial thanks to an unexpected source.

It is now late in the afternoon. There is an urgency about things as the Sabbath began at sunset. Jewish law indicated that those hanged should be taken down and buried before sundown (Deuteronomy 21:23). This was particularly important before the Sabbath.

Roman law said that a criminal lost all rights to a decent burial and it was not unusual for a body to be left on the cross to rot or be eaten by the birds. Jesus was saved from such an indignity by Joseph of Arimathea. Normally a member of the close family, or a disciple, would perform this duty and it was a courageous act on Joseph's behalf to take this initiative.

Arimathea was a village in the hill country of Ephraim, about twenty miles north-west of Jerusalem. Mark tells us that Joseph was a member of the Sanhedrin, the body that condemned Jesus to death. Was he not present when the decision was made? Mark tells us that they all agreed with the decision (14:64). Luke tells us that 'he was a good and upright man who had not consented to their decision and action' (23:50–51). Matthew adds that he had 'become a disciple of Jesus' (27:57:see also John 19:38). Mark simply tells us that he was 'waiting for the kingdom of God'. Joseph's request was tantamount to an admission of support for the condemned Jesus.

Pilate is surprised to hear that Jesus is already dead and Mark alone includes the detail of him reassuring himself that Jesus was really dead. This will be an important detail when the disciples begin to preach the resurrection.

Joseph would have had the help of others, perhaps his servants. John includes Nicodemus in the act of burial (19:39). For the benefit of his Gentile readers Mark gives the details of how Jesus was buried. He makes it clear that the one crucified at the hands of the Jews was given an honourable Jewish burial. The body would have been washed before being placed in the tomb.

Mark tells us that it was a tomb cut out of rock. Matthew adds that it was Joseph's own tomb and new. Luke tells us that it had not been used before, for it was common to place several bodies in such a tomb. A stone is rolled across the entrance.

This may refer to a simple boulder, or some finer tombs would be covered by an elaborate disc-shaped stone about a metre in diameter, like a millstone, which would roll in a groove across the doorway. Such tombs have been discovered dating from the time of Jesus. It would take several men to put such a stone in place or to roll it away again.

Again Mark records the presence of the women. Contemporary Jewish culture would place no value on their testimony, but for Mark their testimony was vital.

Questions

1. What do you make of Joseph of Arimathea? Why do you think he did what he did? Why did he not speak up earlier? Is 'secret discipleship' a real option?

2. There are some who have argued that Jesus never really died; how does Mark meet that objection?

3. What is the significance of the presence of the women throughout these events?

Mark 16:1-8

The stone is rolled away

With the same direct simplicity with which Mark has recorded Jesus' death, he reports his resurrection. As so often in the gospel what God has done leaves people in a state of amazement.

Although Jesus had often spoken of his resurrection, his followers had clearly failed to understand what he had been saying. The disciples lock themselves away secretly (John 20:19) and the women come to offer their last respects. When the Sabbath is over, that is, after sunset, Mary Magdalene and the others bring spices to anoint Jesus' body. It was Jewish custom to do this and was for them a final act of devotion. They did not expect the body to be missing!

Early the next day they make their way to the tomb. Only Mark records their brief conversation on the way. 'How will they remove the stone from the entrance?' They would not have known about the special seal or the armed guard posted by the Sanhedrin (Matthew 27:62–66). It was far harder to remove such a large stone once it was slotted in the prepared groove. But what they could not do God had already done!

They arrive to find the stone rolled aside. Mark does not tell us how it happened, simply that it had. Inside the tomb were inner chambers with small entrances in which a body would be laid. As they make their way in, they are startled by the presence of a 'young man dressed in a white robe'. The word Mark uses can mean simply 'a young man' (cf. 14:51), but his dress implies a supernatural being. Matthew states directly that it was 'an angel of the Lord' (28:2). Their immediate reaction is one of absolute fear.

Mark uses a word that only he uses in the New Testament; it carries a sense of dread as well as amazement.

The angel tries to put their minds at rest. The body has not been stolen, they have not come to the wrong tomb, the simple truth is that the crucified Jesus of Nazareth is no longer there but risen from the dead. Almost like the wording of a telegram the message is given: 'Don't be afraid (stop), He has risen (stop), He is not here (stop)'. The message of Easter morning is not simply that the tomb is empty, but that Jesus is alive.

The women are told to go and tell the disciples the good news, with a special word for Peter, who has not been mentioned by Mark since his repeated denial of Jesus in the courtyard. It is a token of the forgiveness that Peter now knew he enjoyed as he recalled these events to Mark. The promise that he would meet them in Galilee is given in 14:27, immediately before Peter's fated boast, 'Even if all fall away, I will not', and Jesus' honest warning, 'Before the cock crows twice you will disown me three times'. It is fitting that Peter should be on stage as Mark's drama draws to a close.

But it is with the women that the story ends and with the note of wonder and amazement that is so familiar in Mark's gospel. In 1:27, they are amazed at his authority; in 2:12 and 7:37, they are amazed at his healing power; in 4:41 at his power over nature; in 5:20 at his power over demons; in 10:24, 11:18, 12:17, they are amazed at his teaching; in 10:32 at his conviction that he must die; and in 15:5 Pilate is amazed at his silence. Overwhelming wonder is a natural human reaction to the life and ministry of Jesus Christ. It is not surprising that the truth that he is alive should prompt the same response.

Questions

1. If it was Mark's intention to finish his gospel at verse 8, in what way would it have been an appropriate ending? Is the gospel story complete? If you were writing a gospel where would you end the story?

2. What is the significance of the special mention of Peter in verse 7.

3. If Mark's gospel had been lost what would be missing from our understanding of Jesus? What is distinctive about Mark's portrait of Jesus?

An unfinished gospel?

Mark's gospel leaves us with a puzzle. The most reliable manuscripts end at verse 8 and the account ends dramatically in mid-sentence. The style of verses 9–20 is very different from the rest of the gospel and they appear to be a summary of various resurrection appearances added later by another writer.

Why does Mark's gospel end so abruptly? Was he interrupted before he could finish? Mark wrote in days of intense opposition and persecution; could it have been that at this point the knock came on the door and the gospel remained unfinished?

Perhaps the last part of the papyrus has been torn off in very early years. Neither Matthew nor Luke, who used Mark in the composition of their gospels, seem to have known the lost ending. It has been suggested that John 21 may preserve some of it.

Two 'endings' have been given to the gospel. The 'shorter ending' occurs in some later manuscripts and reads 'But they reported briefly and those with him all that they had been told. And after this, Jesus himself sent out, by means of them, from east to west, the saved and imperishable proclamation of eternal salvation'. It doesn't sound like John Mark! The longer ending is found in the NIV margin.

But maybe Mark intended to stop here. It ties in with the repeated note of astonishment and fear that is in the gospel.

We respond to the empty tomb with joy and celebration because we are familiar with its truth but an immediate reaction of overwhelming amazement is quite understandable. The disciples' first response was not one of joy but fear. John tells of them locked away for fear of the Jews and a week later they are still behind locked doors (John 20:19, 26). The early Christians were not a gullible group of wishful thinkers who were easily led or readily convinced. No-one had ever risen from the dead before. It seemed so strange – so unbelievable! It took time before they could take the amazing truth on board.

So Mark's gospel ends with a preposition, 'for' or 'therefore'. Perhaps it is deliberately open-ended, as if Mark is saying 'It's over to you now, it's up to you to complete the story.'

A risen Lord?

What exactly was the evidence of the women? That Jesus had risen? No, not really, it was that the tomb was empty. This is one of the agreed facts of that first Easter Sunday. The Roman guards, the Jewish authorities and everyone who has checked it for themselves agree that the tomb was empty.

Some try to discredit the evidence by pointing to the discrepancies between the gospel accounts. For example, Matthew writes of an angel, whereas John has two. Mark says it was a young man, whereas Luke has two men. Conflicting details like this are easily understood by the sheer trauma of the events. The shock of the three women as they each tell their story would naturally have led to a garbled report. But they all agree that the tomb was empty.

Could they have gone to the wrong tomb? Mary Magdalene and Mary the mother of James had seen him buried (15:47). It is not possible that they would both have been mistaken.

The natural first question to cross their minds would have been, 'Have we come to the right place?' The angel assures them that they have.

Did someone remove the body? The question is who? The official story was that the disciples had done so (Matthew 28:13). But could they have done? They were frightened, demoralised men and the tomb was heavily guarded. Moreover would they have done? In days to come they would preach with convincing power that Jesus was alive. Would their message have carried such conviction if they knew it was a fraud? Would so many of them have been prepared to die a martyr's death for a lie?

Perhaps the authorities removed the body? But it would have been the easiest thing in the world to discredit the whole Christian movement by simply producing the body as irrefutable evidence. Surely they would have done so if they could have done so.

The clear evidence of Mark's abrupt ending is that the tomb was empty and the only satisfactory explanation is that what the angel said is true: 'He has risen!'

Mark 16:9–20

Coda: resurrection appearances

In these closing verses a patchwork of events that took place after Jesus' resurrection are recorded. An unknown writer 'rounds off' the gospel.

The earliest commentary on Mark's gospel (sixth century AD) stops at 16:8. It is generally agreed that verses 9–20 were added later in order to 'complete' the story. Early church authorities like Eusebius (*c.* 265–*c.* 339) and Jerome (*c.* 345–*c.* 419) did not consider them to be authentic. The style and language are certainly not those of John Mark. One tenth-century manuscript attributes them to 'the presbyter Ariston', about whom we know very little! These verses were, however, attached to Mark's gospel very early in the church's history.

A parallel could be drawn with the account of the woman caught in the act of adultery recorded in John 8:1–11, another early tradition that may well be genuine but does not belong to the gospel text as it stands. These verses from Mark's gospel, although written by Mark, clearly go back a long way and are true to the message of the gospel. They are, for the most part, a brief resumé of resurrection appearances that are recorded more fully in the other gospels.

Verses 9–11 summarise the appearance of the risen Christ to Mary, recorded in Luke 24:1–11 and John 20:11–18. Verses 12 and 13 refer to the experience of the two on the road to Emmaus, recorded in Luke 24:13–35. The reference to 'a different form' may explain whey they did not recognise him at first, or it may refer simply to a different form from the one in which Jesus appeared to Mary.

The final paragraph (verses 14–20) reflects the contents of Matthew 28:16–20 and Luke 24:36–50, Jesus' commission to his disciples.

211

Three distinctive strands are worth noting from the verses:

The unbelief of the disciples   The early Christians were not easily convinced of the truth of the resurrection. They refuse to believe Mary Magdalene (verse 11) and the two on the road (verse 13). Unbelief has been a continuing problem for the disciples (e.g. 9:19). They cannot begin to preach the message until they are believers themselves.

The importance of baptism (verse 16)   Baptism is the proper outward expression of inward faith. But notice it is those who do not believe who are condemned, not those who have not been baptised.

The promise of signs and wonders   Jesus speaks of the miracles that would be performed in the early church (verses 17–18). Some of these miracles are recorded in Acts, for example, Paul drives out a demon (Acts 16:18); he is unharmed after a snake bite (Acts 28:5); and he heals many who are sick (Acts 28:7). There are no New Testament examples of Christians drinking poison and surviving.

Verse 19 summarises the ascension of Christ, greater detail being given in Acts 1; and verse 20 seems to be a one-verse summary of the whole of the Acts of the Apostles! The implication is – the story goes on. This is not the end. The risen Lord is still working in and through his people.

Questions

1. Why do you think the first disciples found it so hard to believe that Jesus was alive? Why do people find it so hard to believe it today?
2. Is baptism essential for salvation? Look at the words of verse 16 carefully. What is the practice of baptism in your church?
3. Should we expect to see signs and miracles when we preach the gospel today? If not, why not? If so, then why don't we?

For further reading

Commentaries on Mark's gospel

Barclay, William (1975) *Daily Study Bible* (St. Andrews Press).

Blanch, Stuart (1989) *Encounters with Jesus* (Hodder).

English, Donald (1992) *The message of Mark* (IVP).

The life and ministry of Jesus

Bruce, F.F. (1983) *The hard sayings of Jesus* (Hodder).

France, R.T. (1989) *Jesus – the Radical* (IVP).

Guthrie, Donald (1972) *Jesus the Messiah* (Zondervan).

Stewart, James (1977) *The life and teaching of Jesus Christ* (St. Andrews Press).

Wenham, David (1989) *The Parables of Jesus* (Hodder).

EZRA AND NEHEMIAH

Dave Cave

Free to build

Crossway Bible Guides

The books of Ezra and Nehemiah are powerful examples of God's care for his people. His equipping of leaders for his people is as vital and dynamic today as in Old Testament times. We see how

* leading in God's way brings lasting results
* obeying God restores his blessing
* trusting God defeats the opposition

Crossway Bible Guides are designed for personal devotion and for group-study leaders and members. They give a concise summary and lively application of each passage. They help us grasp the message of the Bible, and, more important, help the Bible get a grip on us.

A useful resource for personal Bible reading and group studies –
Michael Green

Evangelical Alliance is delighted to join together with Crossway in publishing this new series –
Clive Calver

Individuals or groups could find great benefit from this series. Major points are highlighted followed by uncompromising and sharp questions –
Donald English

These guides will facilitate, stimulate and enrich your discovery of God's Word –
Roger Forster

Dave Cave is the leader of Anfield Road Fellowship, near Liverpool football stadium. A Spring Harvest and much-used conference speaker and radio broadcaster, he lives with his wife Tina and their family in inner-city Liverpool.

ACTS

Stephen Gaukroger

Free to live

Crossway Bible Guides

Series Editor for the New Testament: Ian Coffey

Acts is one of the most exciting and relevant Bible books for Christians today. It shows us God powerfully at work in the early church.

This invaluable study guide enables us to find out how Acts speaks to us now. There is plenty of application, so that we can put into practice the lessons we learn in each study.

The Crossway Bible Guides are specially designed for home-group study and for readers at all levels of ability.
Each section has:
  A detailed explanation of the passage
  Questions for group and personal study.

Some sections also have special features that explain complex passages in greater depth.

Stephen Gaukroger is one of Britain's best-known speakers, and the author of bestsellers such as *It Makes Sense*. The Senior Minister of a church in Bedfordshire, he was the youngest ever elected President of the Baptist Union. He and his wife Janet have three children.

1 PETER

Andrew Whitman

Free to hope

Crossway Bible Guides

The apostle Peter encourages us to have hope in all circumstances because

* ⋆ God's love for us is sure
* ⋆ God is always in control
* ⋆ God is in charge of the future

Crossway Bible Guides are designed for personal devotion and for group-study leaders and members. They give a concise summary and lively application of each passage. They help us grasp the message of the Bible, and more important, help the Bible get a grip on us.

A useful resource for personal Bible reading and group studies –
Michael Green

Evangelical Alliance is delighted to join together with Crossway in publishing this new series –
Clive Calver

Individuals or groups could find great benefit from this series. Major points are highlighted followed by uncompromising and sharp questions –
Donald English

These guides will facilitate, stimulate and enrich your discovery of God's Word –
Roger Forster

Andrew Whitman is the pastor of Godmanchester Baptist Church, near Huntingdon, where he lives with his family.